THE MAIN OF LIGHT

THE MAIN
OF LIGHT

On the Concept of Poetry

JUSTUS BUCHLER

New York
Oxford University Press
London   1974   Toronto

Copyright © 1974 by Justus Buchler
Library of Congress Catalogue Card Number: 73-87621
Printed in the United States of America

To
Samuel Buchler

ACKNOWLEDGMENTS

I thank Leonard Feldstein, Richard Kuhns, Robert Olson, Evelyn Shirk, Beth Singer, and Victorino Tejera for reading the manuscript. Their critical comments have been very useful to me.

I also thank the publishers and persons who have granted me the permission needed for quotation from certain copyrighted works. The details regarding such permission are specified in the Notes at the back of the book.

J. B.

November 1972

CONTENTS

Introduction   3

I   The Apologetic and Eulogistic Tradition   7

II   Feeling and the "Inner World"   22

III   The Idea of Concreteness   50

IV   On Various Contrasts of Poetry and Prose   73

V   Poetic Judgment and Poetic Query   87

VI   Ontological Parity and the Sense of
      Prevalence   117

VII   Knowledge, Actuality, and Analysis
      in Poetry   148

      Notes   174

      Index   181

THE MAIN OF LIGHT

Nativity, once in the main of light,
Crawls to maturity, wherewith being crown'd,
Crooked eclipses 'gainst his glory fight.
                                    Shakespeare, Sonnet 60

INTRODUCTION

My chief purpose in this book is to attain better philosophic understanding of an elusive domain of art. I hesitate to think of how many efforts there have been to clarify "the nature of poetry." Their ostensible variety, and what I cannot help feeling to be their philosophic inadequacy, accentuate the magnitude of the problem. The subject-matter called "theory of poetry," very much like "theory of knowledge" and "theory of language," is most often pursued as if it were quite separate from systematized philosophic reflection. I am not of the opinion that when so pursued it must lack importance or usefulness. But a philosophic attempt to define poetry has to concern itself with the kind of human utterance that poetry is. And this in turn requires that we become clear, or at least clearer, about the concept of utterance or judgment, which is wider and philosophically more basic than the concept of language. The outlook on human judgment that I first formulated during the late 1940's in my classes at Columbia was engendered by a number of convictions at which I had arrived. One of them was that poetic utterance, and artistic utterance in general, had simply never been dealt with satisfactorily on the foundational level.

It has not been part of my purpose to review poetic theory, or

to seek out everything written on the subject. Nor am I con-
cerned with literary history, with movements and schools, with
the practice of literary criticism, or with what professional stu-
dents of literature call "poetics." In order to show what has been
impeding an adequate conception of poetry, it is not necessary to
select for discussion representatives of every cultural period or
literary trend. Certain unaccountably persistent ideas and alle-
giances are what need to be represented.

The first four of the following chapters deal with these ideas
and allegiances, and with the issues to which they are customarily
tied. The issues as issues stand in great need of clarification and
resolution. One of the objectives of these first four chapters is to
engage a group of ideas rendered sacrosanct by long tradition,
functioning without vitality, often without meaning, and with
the force only of slogans; ideas hardened into a sterile language.
The language remains undiminished in its sway. It continues to
talk about poetry in terms of "the imagination," "reality,"
"unity," "inner experience," "form and content," and the like.
The philosophic temper permeating these grooves of thought
needs to be carefully examined not merely because it inhibits a
fresh conception of the nature of poetry and continues to harbor
false generalizations, but because at this point in time it tends
to stultify philosophic thinking as such. An examination is
largely what the first four chapters are devoted to, although it
includes in its compass conceptions which are less traditional
but equally wanting.

The earlier chapters demonstrate the need, the later chapters
attempt the construction, of a just theory of poetry. The critical
strain is subordinated in the later chapters but not abandoned.
The just theory aims, as the expression goes, to be "faithful" to
the practice and variations of the art. Such fidelity ultimately lies
in a theory's directive power, its ability not merely to ascertain
pattern in the various manifestations of poetry but to enhance
the identifying grasp, the awareness, of each manifestation. So,
it is not merely a matter of "fitting" all the instances of poetry,

as if each were already a satisfactorily identifiable unit, but of illuminating what it means to be an instance of poetry.

Of the concepts that Chapters V–VII introduce, all are intended to promote a more viable philosophic language. Some belong to a metaphysics of the human process; others belong to a metaphysics wider in scope, a general ontology. Both sets of concepts are equally involved in the account. Chapter V provides for poetry an elemental location, a terrain; elemental in the sense that poetry is not the sole inhabitant, and in the sense that, along with much else near to it and far from it, poetry is a specific kind of human complex. Within this sphere basic distinctions are made, enabling us to determine unique traits of poetry amidst common ones. Chapter VI formulates traits which, in a definite respect, are central: it is to them that we must turn most emphatically in order to differentiate the poetic product from any other. Chapter VII, besides drawing some far-reaching consequences from the reflections of V and VI, shows, by reconsidering certain classical values (knowledge, analysis) often held to be absent from poetry, that on the contrary they cannot fail to be present.

It would not be quite accurate to say that the first four of our chapters show how poetry is not to be conceived, and the last three how poetry is to be conceived. For along with the criticisms made in I–IV reasons are given, and superior positions are indicated or anticipated; guiding concepts are already at work. And similarly, the theory developed in V-VII arrives at its component formulations partly through the use, along the way, of contrasting views, some of which emanate from views earlier criticized. It would be more accurate, then, to think of the book as offering certain concepts and principles which are in process of being enunciated throughout: in the first half of the book they function informally, sometimes implicitly, and are operative in the service of criticism; in the second half, they are augmented, generalized, and formally articulated.

The writers with whom I have chosen to contend at greatest

length or recurrently (where contention is necessary) for the
most part meet a twofold criterion: they are dominated by the
ideas and attitudes to which I have alluded, and they argue along
philosophic (or quasi-philosophic) lines. They interest me as in-
dividuals who reason in their own way: it does not matter to me
what "ism" or how many isms they have been forced to stand
for historically. Their number could have been very much en-
larged; and if the selective condition of arguing philosophically
were disregarded, that number could have been enlarged indefi-
nitely. At certain points I have dealt in a somewhat unkere-
monious way with positions or formulations put forth by
writers whom I otherwise admire. Any one of these positions
may or may not be representative of its author's work as a whole.
But because it is representative of a significant trend in the con-
ception of poetry, I have felt obliged to single it out sharply.

Although this essay restricts itself to the search for essential
characteristics of poetry, the restriction in no way denies the
importance of other types of interests or emphases, say upon
diversity of values, forms of meaning, or social and psychological
conditions of utterance, in the poetic process and in its products.
Unless I am much mistaken, however, the concepts framed in the
following pages are relevant to investigations stemming from
such interests.

This book is related to four others.* They provide the broader
philosophic context for the views it contains, as well as alterna-
tive or detailed treatment of certain ideas applied in it. But it is
written to stand on its own and to extend the structure that it
represents.

---

* *Toward a General Theory of Human Judgment* (1951), *Nature and Judg-
ment* (1955), *The Concept of Method* (1961), and *Metaphysics of Natural
Complexes* (1966). These were published by Columbia University Press.

I

THE APOLOGETIC
AND EULOGISTIC
TRADITION

i

A large amount of poetic theory, from earliest times to the present, approaches its subject in the following way: "You ask what is poetry? Poetry is the most wonderful of all things. It is divine. It is the begetter of all meaning, all knowledge, all value; it is the mother of all civilization. What other activity of man can delight us so much, please us so intensely?" This type of approach is reactive, defensive, apologetic. Its exaggerations are symptomatic of its fears. It flourishes in cultures where the arts as practiced by individuals are vulnerable to individual criticism and social distrust. The art of poetry in particular bears the burden of employing as its most obvious medium language, about which everyone is intuitively expert. Thus poets have been readily branded as liars not by philistines alone but by responsible critics who condone their "fictions" as the natural cost of a high purpose. The art celebrated since classical antiquity as first among arts is the art distinguished by a historical parade of Defences and Apologies.

No great power of argumentation is needed to see that the nervously enthusiastic treatment of the concept of poetry does far more harm than good, so far as understanding is concerned.

Even if its account of poetry's effects were moderated, its irrele-
vance to the many questions at issue would be patent. Words-
worth's famous characterization of poetry as "the breath and
finer spirit of all knowledge . . . the impassioned expression
which is in the countenance of all Science" exemplifies the eulo-
gistic tradition; [1] and so does Boccaccio's statement that "what-
ever is composed as under a veil, and thus exquisitely wrought,
is poetry and poetry alone." [2] The approach preserved by this
tradition is responsible for what J. W. Mackail calls "splendid
tributes . . . paid to poetry by its lovers under the guise of a
definition." [3] The authors of these tributes have included men of
discernment and depth who cannot be regarded simply as the
victims of a cultural tradition. Their critical rhetoric is frequently
marked by strong insight. Their overstatement yields a fund of
instructive confusions.

Shelley, whose torrential eulogism is intertwined with strains
of philosophic acuteness, develops his outlook in a manner partly
olympian and partly analytical. Poetry, he says, is "connate with
the origin of man."

[In the] infancy of society every author is necessarily a poet, because
language itself is poetry.

Poets, moreover,

are not only the authors of language and of music, of the dance, and
architecture, and statuary, and painting; they are the institutors of
laws and the founders of civil society, and the inventors of the arts of
life, and the teachers, who draw into a certain propinquity with the
beautiful and the true, that partial apprehension of the agencies of the
invisible world which is called religion.

All of this emanates from the state of historically primordial man.

In the youth of the world, men dance and sing and imitate natural ob-
jects, observing in these actions, as in all others, a certain rhythm or
order.[4]

Those who react to the varieties of "rhythm or order" most sensitively, who link them resourcefully with pleasure, especially the highest pleasure of "approximation to the beautiful," are the poets. Their language is "vitally metaphorical; that is, it marks the before unapprehended relations of things and perpetuates their apprehension." What, after all, was the task of the primitive? To turn human power into human accomplishment. The herculean (poetic) beginning lay, and each beginning lies, in discerning the "similitudes" of things and uniting them. This is the function of "imagination." Accordingly, poetry in the most basic sense "may be defined as 'the expression of the imagination.' "

It is no longer necessary to deride the a priori anthropology and history typical in this manner of thinking. The mythical account can even be tolerated as providing a scheme for the central ideas. But it is in these ideas that the trouble has lurked before and after Shelley. From a state of man in which "language itself is poetry" we cannot simply whisk to a state in which it is metaphorical language that is poetry. Nor can we cover up by saying that in the beginning all language, after all, was metaphorical. The theory may require us to say it, but the theory does not allow us to say it. The metaphorical is the linking of things according to their similitudes. It is the expression of the "imagination." But Shelley, in order to define imagination, distinguishes between imagination and reason. Reason "respects the differences of things." Reason and imagination *both* define the human animal. Not all language, then, can be poetry. And poets cannot be the "authors of language." And if we wish to say that poetry arose when man arose, we must mean that it but not it alone arose; for there is nothing compelling us to believe that, of the two contrasting forms of "mental action" known as reason and imagination, either is prior to the other, in origin or in importance.

At this point it is possible to see, with respect to imagination, an unexpressed diremption in Shelley and in much of poetic theory. On the one hand, a profound impulse suggests that imagination (hence, "poetry") is the source of all art, law, society, religion, philosophy, and science (taking "science" in both its broader and narrower sense). Yet on the other hand, imagination, if it is to be *a* power, a *distinguishable* power within the many-ness of human functioning, cannot be the source of *all* that is human. Again, on the one hand, imagination underlies what is called creativity; but on the other hand, it is associated by poetic theorists with the creation only of the true and the beautiful, and not the creation of *all* that is human, including the false, the hurt-ful, the ugly, the mendacious. On the one hand, the imagination is seen as the source of the good that is to be found in human life; yet, on the other, we cannot help thinking of it as a pre-carious and limited force, lost if it is not victorious over other human forces such as the unimaginative, and meaningless if it is not complemented by the non-imaginative. On the one hand, the primordial "author" is seen as necessarily a poet, for poetry is to be found in language as such. On the other, we cannot preserve our scrupulousness if we do not think of poetry as achieved methodically rather than poured forth by the mere act of speaking. On the one hand, we are impelled to link poetry, imagination, and the good. Yet on the other, we cannot in conscience think of "poetry" and "good poetry" as identical in meaning: no greater offense to the idea of goodness can be committed than to treat it as an ornamental and empty qualifica-tion. It is worth dwelling for a moment upon this last confusion between the nature of a discipline, or the conditions of its pro-ductivity, and the merit of its products. Along with making "good" a vacuous word, it makes assessment in terms of degree meaningless. The number of offenders here is large, and they include even Coleridge. Nothing, of course, prevents us from saying that poetry as such is good, in the sense that poetic pro-duction and activity is good even if, in some instances of such activity, bad poems result. Further, good poetry may be written by evil men, or put to evil uses; and bad poetry may be put to good uses, say in good songs, or in the teaching of poetic craft. The main point, in any case, is that the goodness of the poetic enterprise does not imply that only good poetry is poetry. The nature of the art is one matter, the evaluation of its output is another.

The heavy reliance on "imagination" as somehow explanatory of poetry makes it necessary to amplify one of the foregoing points. Imagination is thought of as a key because of its endless promise of novel products, its unpredictable magic. So immersed are the "imaginationists" in the mysteriously compelling force of poetry that they fail to see the imaginative process dispassionately. Some of them (who take seriously the provocative reflections of both Kant and Coleridge on imagination) do recognize that there is a mathematical and a legal and a philosophic imagination no less "imaginative" than the poetic, even if they assign to the latter an underlying, seminal primacy. What they do not recognize is that imagination can be destructive, contrary to the spirit of poetry, and contrary to the spirit of invention in any of its forms. Imagination envisions and begets the gas chambers, the ingenious plans of warfare that exterminate millions, the techniques of moral suppression that intimidate the living millions. Coleridge, applying his view of imagination to the work of the poet, says that the poet "diffuses a tone and spirit of unity, that blends, and (as it were) *fuses* [man's faculties] each into each, by that synthetic and magical power," which accomplishes, most fundamentally, a "balance or reconcilement of opposite or discordant qualities."[5] Whether through the ironies wrought by passing time or through initial imprecision, this definition of function no longer applies to poetry uniquely. Magic can be evil magic. The diffusion of a spirit of unity that blends men's powers and reconciles opposite qualities can be the work of a diabolical social imagination that achieves a deadly oneness. The fusing of men's faculties may destroy the vitality as well as the independent functioning of each, and may prevent each from complementing or correcting the direction of the others. If, as a sheer power actualized, imagination "bodies forth the forms of things unknown," it is not hard to see why it can be the domain of lunatics. We need to know more about the domain peculiar to poets.

The notion that poetry is the heart of imagination is near kin to another, which has it that poetry is related to "the whole man." In Coleridge's words, "the poet . . . brings the whole soul of man into activity." We may assume that this applies both to the poet and to the man who assimilates poetry. The connection between the view that poetry is the human simulacrum of divine creativity and this view, that poetry activates all human powers, is (painfully) clear. To create so much is indeed to require every power available, not to mention the grace of God. And this view, like the other, has awesome but not very edifying consequences. Man, or the soul of man, is a kind of being with mixed potentialities, potentialities for beneficence and love or for vileness and savagery. What, then, can be meant by the idea in question? When the poet activates the whole man, does he activate an infinite maelstrom of qualities? And does he then somehow, from all this, distil products with limited substance, with specific content? Does he, as poet, activate the whole soul by bringing into play every one of the "mental operations" which philosophers have tried to enumerate? (When all philosophers of note are taken into account, the main operations described are found to be mercifully small in number and not too diversely conceived.) Does the poet activate the whole soul in each poem or in his career as poet, and regardless of whether he writes three or three thousand poems? Does the poet aim, within his lifetime, to express or to provoke every possible human twist of feeling, every conceivable "passion of the soul"—including, let us say, the passion for sliced roast lamb on garlic toast? The idea of activating the whole man and the whole soul is difficult, to say the least. But is there, perhaps, a simple essential wholeness, a unitary indivisible humanness which the poet brings to bear on all that enters into his poetry? In any case, no such idea has ever been made intelligible.

Santayana, in his version of the whole-soul theme, says that "the poet must draw the whole soul into his harmonies." [6] Does he mean that otherwise the poet is a lesser poet or no poet? Is he implying that anything less than the whole soul—perish the thought of measuring the difference—will not produce "harmonies"? Why do we rarely find such legislative advice given to the scientist? No one feels quite so free to tell him what he "must" do.

Poetry, Paul Valéry believes, "must extend over the whole being; it stimulates the muscular organization by its rhythms . . . ." This physiological theme, which seems to suggest that poetry is good exercise, presumably for poet and reader alike, sounds like a novel variation in the "whole-man" tradition, but it is entailed in the general principle, as Valéry's sequel reveals:

Poetry aims to arouse or reproduce the unity and harmony of the living person, an extraordinary unity that shows itself when a man is possessed by an intense feeling that leaves none of his powers disengaged.[7]

Is it not rather remarkable that "the unity of the living person" should be accounted "an extraordinary unity"? For this virtually implies that prior to poetry the living person lacks the "unity" that is ordinarily and even truistically assigned to him as an organism and that serves as the model for the notion of "organic unity" so dear to the poetic ideal of philosophers like Aristotle and Hegel. But what is more immediately pertinent at this point is the view that poetry has its true effect on a man when it "leaves none of his powers disengaged."

A sobering thought; a frightening one. But part of a trend of loose thinking in the eulogistic tradition. According to Hazlitt, a century before, all true poetry "rouses the whole man within us." [8] Alas, that it should rouse the whole man, and not rather the good man, the sensitive man, the understanding, loving, appreciative, grateful man alone. Why should the dishonest, the arrogant, the contemptuous, the tired strains within us; the cheap, commercial, envious, murderous, brutal impulses be aroused by poetry? Of course, there is no reason to believe the idea. There is reason only to believe that criticism can be infected by a concept that sounds right and comes to nothing. But trying again to penetrate the meaning of the whole-man slogan, suppose that the expression "whole man" is taken not as synonymous with "all that there is and can be in man" or "everything in man considered together" but, instead, as meaning a unique overarching "quality of wholeness in man." Yet, should we not ask what this quality might be and how we might recognize it? Surely it cannot be another of the "indescribables"; there are too many of them, and there is no room for any more. This time, in the throes of the whole-man idea, it might be candid to say that we don't know, or even, that we don't know what we are looking for.

ii

The idea that poetry is deeply rooted in the life of early man has an irresistible appeal. Santayana's view that "Primitive poetry is the basis of all discourse" [9] sounds but is not more extreme than Hegel's, that poetry is older than artistic prose. Both views make facile transitions back and forth between a speculative anthropology and a philosophic comparison of poetry and prose. For Santayana there is a "descent from poetry to prose." For Hegel poetry is "the original" grasp of truth, a form of knowledge in which no distinction is made or needed between universal and particular. Both feel that the usual process of dealing with universal or general ideas, namely abstracting, is a later development; and both deal with the problems which this development is thought to bring.

Despite the fact that we have here two philosophers of the most fearless breed, the apologetic strain is unquestionably present and not difficult to recognize. Poetry, bewildering both to the men of plain good sense and the busy men of industry and intellect, is attributed to the primal consciousness of their ancestors, who remain happily anonymous but who are made to excel them by bearing a heroic role in the early stage of human development. Even so, the speculative dispositions of Hegel and Santayana differ strikingly. Hegel sees poetry as having a vital function in early human history, awaiting its destiny in the cosmic drama, where cognitive consciousness unfolds and moves toward its own consummation. Santayana sees poetry as fundamental because it is the embodiment of childlike irresponsibility, of boundless freedom; because its essential activity is telling delightful lies, "fancying how creation might have moved upon other lines." Both philosophers, in their modes of evolutionary explanation, are committed to hierarchical schemes, schemes at once temporal and methodological, whereby one human discipline is better than another in such-and-such a way, and the other better than the first in such-and-such another way, and the two of them inferior or superior to yet another. The general result is an uneven fluctuation between insight and dogma, especially where poetry is concerned; for since no other form of expression is so baffling, the challenge to speculative ingenuity encourages an attempt to domesticate that form by means of apt classification.

According to Hegel, poetry "has been the most universal and cosmopolitan instructor of the human race and is so still." [10] Like the ancients, he considers it the supreme art, and in his own characteristic manner he calls it the attainment of the highest possibilities of art as art. He sees each art as having its unique excellence, but he requires us to accept the view that art in general entails the attainment of definite ideals or perfections. And we are required to believe that these generic perfections are not attainable by each art in its own way, but by certain arts more than by others, and more by one art than by any other. The possible values of art are not, therefore, shown to be what they are just because they are severally manifested by the various arts. They include overarching values which a given art may or may not fully realize, and which are manifested in a hierarchy of the arts. Poetry occupies the apex. It is not only greatest in its artistic perfection; it is "the universal art." This means to Hegel that it

is capable of reclothing and expressing under every conceivable mode every content (*Inhalt*) that can possibly enter or proceed from the imagination (*Phantasie*) of man.

No other art has the scope of poetry. Of no other art can it be said that "every content, every sort of spiritual or natural fact" falls within its domain and is within the scope of its powers. One direct and intended implication is that poetry can do much of what other arts can do, while other arts can do relatively little of what poetry can do. Poetry, also identified by Hegel as the art of language or speech, is the art best able to grasp in ideational form what he calls "the innermost actuality of conscious life," the "life of Spirit."

The principle governing the supposed hierarchy within the realm of art is derived by Hegel from the consideration of other, more general principles. There is, in his view, a broader, more extensive hierarchy. Art itself, poetry and all, is ultimately inferior, so far as truth and knowledge are concerned, to religion and philosophy. In a way, the highest tribute given to poetry is that it tends strongly to overflow its proper boundaries and thus brings art to the very border of religion and philosophy. This does not mean that poetry should violate its essential artistic concern, which requires it to deal with the world of sense, however it may transform that world. It means, rather, that poetry has the power to transcend itself, a power, among others, which explains its location at the apex of art. If we try to detach ourselves from this Hegelian scheme and try to consider, within the life of art, what justification can be mustered for the kind of procedure which evaluates poetry in relation to the other arts, we are bound to be struck by an interesting form of arbitrariness. But of course from the Hegelian viewpoint such an attempt at detachment is illegitimate and abortive. And we should have to concede the justice of the view that we cannot become detached from fundamentals: the dissent must be from what is conceived as fundamental.

Aside from Hegel's commitment to a principle of the "limits" of art as such, there is a distinct similarity in temper between his view that the content of poetry is "the collective art of the world of ideas elaborated by the imagination" and Shelley's conception of poetry as "the expression of the imagination." Despite differences in their sense of what imagination includes, or where it is exemplified, the intent in both formulations is to regard poetry as a paragon of imaginative activity.

Now if we think of poetry itself, and forget for a moment its status among the arts, we can appreciate a salutary strain in Hegel's opinion that it is able to deal with every possible "content." This opinion appears to be far less arbitrary than one which finds poetry able to deal only with such-and-such kinds of things, with the kinds that science "cannot" deal with, and not with the kinds that science deals with most "successfully." But more pressing at this point is the question why this liberal view of poetry's domain cannot be applied to any other of the "fine arts." Why cannot any possible subject or theme or idea fall within the scope of any art? Why cannot painting or music "express" or "represent" or "deal with" or "reclothe" whatever is dealt with by poetry? One answer is that the other arts are limited by their "media"—the various kinds of sensory materials with which they work and by which their powers are in a high degree determined. Poetry, Hegel believes, has as its medium that which is itself sensuous only in an incidental way and which is able to provide an indefinite range for expression, namely language. Thus the sound of speech is not fundamental but only accessory to the ideas which speech sets forth (ideas *relating* to the world of sensory phenomena). This bias toward language as the "medium" which is of highest value and greatest power is shared by Hegel with Aristotle, Shelley, and most other people.

Presumably, in language almost any "content" can be expressed. But most particularly, Hegel thinks, no art compares with the art of language in respect of expounding that content, making it explicit.

The confusions that permeate this view and appear to justify belief in a single absolute scale on which all expressive power is to be measured, rest on a clandestine assumption that all expression is a kind of language. The widespread conception of an art as "saying," as saying what it has to say, betrays this assumption. The "rank" of the arts is thus estimated in the terms that one of them provides. By its own measuring-rod the art of language proves its own superior versatility and universality. Instead of wondering whether the notion of dealing with or expressing a content involves one and the same criterion of determination in all the arts, Hegel feels quite secure about the standard of expressiveness. His aim is to ascertain the comparative power of each art to grasp and develop a content.

Prizing the comparative power of an art to expound and expose a content is based on a type of expectation pertinent in the area of language, though actually of very questionable pertinence in the area of poetic language. Talking and naming, as human powers, are no doubt deliverable with expediency and dispatch. They are "flashier" types of expression and can accomplish quantitatively large products quickly. But mere language is not the art of language, any more than a splash of paint is the art of painting. The problems of poetry in manipulating its "medium" are not fewer than those of the other arts. The finitude and determinateness that inhere in the various artistic media inhere in language as well. To speak of finitude by no means implies that we can rule a priori on what it is that the art of language or any other art can and cannot express. It implies only that we may with good reason respect the specific differences which have permitted us to identify various arts in the first place. Language cannot make a sculpture, any more than marble or clay can make an iambic pentameter. To think of language as "spiritually free" and of other media as sensuously bound is to make a preference clear but hardly to demonstrate a truth about hierarchy in art. Even if we think of language as the dominant mode of social communication—a most dubious assumption unless we rule out innumerable forms of action, assertion, and contrivance besides those of language—a distinction is always in order, between the extent of communication and its value. In the same way, the spontaneous availability of language for purposes of expression is no guarantee of its desirability as the expressive medium under all conditions.

The arts are not related in such a way that they vie with each other in appropriating "contents." The contents are not all or wholly "there" for them to appropriate. To a large extent, a content dealt with in language is itself tacitly determined by the workings of language. A. C. Bradley, in his classic attack on the distinction between "substance" and "form" within a poem, warns against confusing this distinction with that between "subject" and "poem," a distinction which he accepts.[11] But an artistic "subject," too, like any constituent of a work of art, is discovered to be definitively what it is in virtue of the artistic labor. The artist, to be sure, is receptive to the conditions of his world, including ideational stimuli and various structures, whether he wishes to be or not; so that the work is never wholly his. But subjects get redrawn, newly shaped, by the artist's purpose and power. Confidence in the purity of subject-matter amidst the many modes and processes of expression lends itself to emphasizing the primacy of language: subjects are there to be named, described, identified. The process of verbal identification makes it easy to suppose that the subject in its complete integrity precedes artistic activity instead of emerging from such activity as a subject to be identified with greater precision and different significance. It is foolish, of course, to deny that subjects can be grossly identified in advance of artistic labor. It is equally foolish to deny that subjects are re-defined, or defined; or that sometimes they are actually engendered by artistic labor which earlier was directed to an end quite differently envisaged.

Why should we be concerned at all with the question whether music, painting, architecture, or poetry, is explicit—whether it explicates or exposes a content well? If we are ever worried whether the plastic arts, for example, "do justice to a subject," we are in danger of approaching them as if they were quasi-linguistic in character. It is a fair question whether any art at all, including poetry, aims to "explicate" a content, no matter if the content is posed in advance or not. To think of one art as having greater explicative power than another is thus a thorny path to follow. If the arts are to be compared in this respect, how is the criterion of measurement framed? Whence is it derived? How can it be determined whether music has the power in greater or lesser degree than painting? What does it mean to say that a particular content in sculpture can be made more explicit than a particular content in music? If the content be deemed antecedently the same for the two arts, how are the two different types of activity to be measured or compared? If the two arts be deemed to have different contents, on what basis can the power of the two activities be compared independently of their initial inequality? What, then, would we be talking about if we held that a content of poetry can be made more explicit than a content of painting? We cannot equate explicitness and verbal explicitness without begging the question. How, indeed, *within* any art would we determine degree of explicitness? What makes one piece of music more explicit than another? Even within poetry, degree of explicitness is of dubious meaning. To assume its pertinence is to import into the work of poetry a trait the need for which obtains primarily in a very different area of language.

Hegel's principle of the universality of poetry, if it is worth preserving, should be stated, not in the form: poetry can express every possible content, but in the form: there is no specifiable content that poetry cannot deal with. Then it becomes evident that for poetry to deal with a content is for poetry to deal with a content in its own way. Plainly, poetry cannot be expected to deal with ideas in every possible way. When this restatement and qualification of the principle is made, we are able to ask why there should be any specifiable content that arts like painting and music cannot deal with in *their* own ways. The problem of measuring the relative power of expressing content is thus converted into the problem of clarifying essential differences within the artistic mode of utterance.

II

FEELING AND
THE "INNER WORLD"

i

To most people "language" means the kind of language that is theirs. But typically, even those who are said to be "language-conscious," including philosophers, feel that the language of a discipline methodically pursued is obliged to justify its difference from "everyday" language. They want to know why philosophers need to use the terms they use, why the language of poets needs to seem so far removed from the familiar avenues of expression. If they believe, as they usually do, that there is a single standard of linguistic clarity, effectiveness, or honesty, they will be especially impatient with philosophy and poetry. Since philosophers, they feel, differ so much from one another substantively, the language of philosophy as such must be a mass aberration. Poets, notoriously, outdo one another in "obscurity"—a suspicion deepened by the frequent contention of literary critics that poetic language is "untranslatable." The language of science, though equally inaccessible to the average devotee of plain talk, is considered by him to be much more trustworthy, for he assures himself that whatever may be the character of this language, the discipline that underlies it is altogether legitimate and reliable.

Somewhat ironically, the language of poetry has been dis-
trusted both on the grounds that it is indirect and circumlocu-
tory, and on the grounds that it is cryptic or enigmatic. Either
conception has its corollary in the view that science and poetry
cannot both be concerned with the same world. Hence arises the
view that poetry is concerned with the "inner world." And this
is a conclusion that goes down well with the hard-headed guard-
ians of good sense no less than with literary theorists. Sometimes
the inner world is described as the "subjective universe," or as
the world in which the "outer" world is mirrored. The outer
world (or "objective universe") is "mirrored in consciousness, in
the world of spirit." The inner world is also called the world "of
feeling, of experience." [1] There is the inevitable division of opin-
ion as to whether this is a world of "imagination" or a world of
"reality." Some hold it to be "equally real" with the outer world,
and some hold it to be "more real."

The notion of an inner world goes back very far. It cannot
be examined here in the various forms it has assumed. But a few
questions, at least, can be raised with regard to the belief that
such a world is the world in terms of which poetry is to be un-
derstood.

Is there an inner world common to all poets? Or is each poet's
world *his* inner world? Or is every private inner world continu-
ous with every other? Such a continuum of private worlds would
constitute a fairly common world. And if this is the world of
poetry, is it closed to all but poets? Is it, indeed, the world *of*
poetry or the world *for* poetry? In other words, is it accessible
to all but expressible only by poets? Is the inner world there for
poets to enter, or is it there only because there is poetry? Is the
world of actual poetry an outcome of the inner world, a product
of that world? Or is the world of poetry, as constituted by poems
and other linguistic complexes, that which gets to be called
"inner"? What is to be found in the inner world? Is there any-
thing besides the feelings or ideas of the poet—of poets? If there
is nothing but feelings and ideas, what are these feelings or

ideas "about"? To what do they relate? The outer world? Or are
they feelings about other feelings—with no need to trace how
the original feelings arose?

Somehow this inner world of poetry gets transformed into the
language of poetry, which usually is addressed to all, and is
meant to be universally available. Is the language of poetry,
then, the language of the inner world, or is there no "language"
in the inner world? Language presupposes the relatedness of
individuals, including the relation of an individual to himself in
different capacities; and it presupposes a world in which the re-
latedness, including communication, acquires purpose. Must we
say that the individual words of poetic language are the same
words as any others in social use, and therefore represent the
outer world, but that the poetic combinations of these words rep-
resent the inner world? But if so, then in the poetic process ele-
ments belonging to the outer world are used to produce com-
pounds belonging to the inner.

A strange version emanates from Coleridge, though in itself,
and taken as the reaffirmation of a theme beloved in literary
thought and German philosophy, it sounds innocent enough:
"One characteristic belongs to all true poets, that they write from
a principle within, not originating in anything without." [2] This
position seems designed to assure that poetry originates in the
soul, and to rescue the poet from the possible suspicion that he
merely reacts to forces impinging "upon" him. Presumably he
accepts from society a language, and from the outer world the
things he cannot help talking about. He is like the Master of the
Household who carves the turkey. The turkey is not cooked by
him, the knife and the dinnerware are put before him, and he
carves. His is the first ritual stroke, and nothing prior to it counts.
In this manner alone can the poet vie with God. Prior to his art
there are only meaningless specters, like the chaos prior to Crea-
tion. It is not enough that the poet should produce works of art.
They must be bestowed by his grace, and they must be discon-
tinuous with all else, as the inner world is from the outer.

The inner world has been claimed as the habitation of many who are not poets. It has been said, for instance, to be the world of mathematicians. One way in which the difference between the two worlds has been described is, that the outer world is the world of "fact," and the inner world the world of "fancy." The world of fact inhibits us, for we must deal with actualities not of our choice, with "stubborn facts" not of our making. The world of fancy is the world of freedom. There we can produce and do what we will, without constraint. In the world of fact the possibilities are limited; in the world of fancy anything is possible.

The shallowness of this version of the contrast between inner and outer worlds matches the fogginess of the previous one. For in any world, power is exercised and power is limited. What can be "done" in the world of fact is comparable with what can be done in the world of fancy. And what cannot be done in the world of fancy is comparable with what cannot be done in the world of fact. The military conquerors, the political planners, the industrial profiteers need no world of fancy to exercise their power. In the world of fact, a great many things which they did not make they can break. In the world of fancy, a great many things which we make we cannot break. The products of fancy have their integrity. The elements from which they were produced were not themselves all produced. And what is produced cannot be unproduced; the time and the process of its making cannot be undone. The images or ideas we fabricate cannot be wholly recalled or wholly erased, and sometimes cannot be modified. The ideas and images which have sprung from us may dominate us. And just as we often cannot dismiss the products of fancy, so in other cases we cannot retain or hold on to them. Many wildly fabricated images and juxtapositions of traits cannot be preserved in their original vivacity or intensity, or survive the occasion of their birth, despite the exercise of "will." But as often as not, the wild images, the "inner feelings" of the "'inner world," haunt and tyrannize over their producers, again regardless of will or desire. And once more in the other direction, our

fancies typically collapse and disintegrate for lack of emotional
support. Their evanescence is as much due to a problem of dis-
cernment in framing them as their longevity is due to a problem
of self-knowledge and self-governance. The notion that in the
world of fancy we can do "more" than in the world of fact, and
even do what we please, is at bottom based on the erroneous
metaphysical assumption that where pure imagination or pure
thought is concerned the variety of possibilities is unlimited
("anything is possible"). In any set of conditions (in any
"world") there are possibilities and impossibilities. In the world
of fancy golden mountains are possible, but mountains without
valleys are not. Any height may be assigned to a fancied moun-
tain, but we must abide by the traits which make that mountain
a mountain—height as such, slope, a top—and the elimination of
these traits is impossible. The idea of "pure" imagination or
thought is not an exaggeration; it is a confusion.

How can the fact-fancy version of the two worlds be applied
to the poetic process? The most important works which the poet
is said to produce in the world of fancy, the works of poetry,
are not left to remain in that world. Do they enter the world of
fact? Do they, in the world of fact, themselves become "facts"
for the poet's audience? If so, they must also have become facts
for the poet. We must believe that at one moment they are in the
world of freedom, and at another moment in the world of com-
pulsion. Are they, therefore, in the moment before the transition
from one world to the other, the kind of being that is wholly
susceptible of annihilation by fiat, and in the moment after,
wholly determinate and irreversible? In the world of fancy is the
poet free even from his own habituation, personal character, and
methodic direction? Is he at one moment spontaneous and unin-
hibited, and at an adjacent moment bound like Prometheus? And
when others respond to the "fact" of his poetry, so that it is for
them a stubborn actuality not of their making, how is criticism
possible? How can the critic, by simply reacting to a completed
factual whole, contribute to the meaning and the communicative

effect of the poetry? The hypothesis of the two realms makes it more and not less difficult to illuminate the poetic process.

To describe the poet's world as the world of "experience" is conceptually empty. The reason is not merely that the term "experience" has many meanings, all established if not clearly articulated in either common or theoretical usage, and that some of these are incompatible with others even in the face of subtle interpretation, but that none of these established meanings can be regarded as intrinsically more legitimate than any other. Some of these meanings remain useful and hard to get along without. But there is reason to believe, and increasingly as time goes on, that the philosophic usefulness of the term is exhausted. To say that the poet resorts to "experience" is about as clarifying as the parallel saw that the scientist resorts to "experience." The experience of the poet is intended to be contrasted with "fact" (the "objective"). The experience of the scientist is intended to be contrasted with "fancy" (the "subjective"). *Everyone* resorts to "experience"; nor is it necessary to "resort." In one sense or another, in one respect or another, everyone experiences. Sooner or later it is evident that those who speak of the poet's world as the world of "experience" neatly entrap themselves. For inevitably, in seeking to reinforce the integrity of this domain, they also call it "inner experience," thereby implicitly accepting "outer experience" as equally experiential and therefore equally relevant to the designs of the poet.

One other instance of how poetic theory can be garbled by the notion of experience will suffice. According to Santayana, the poet "initiates us, by feigning something which, as an experience is impossible, into the meaning of the experience which we have actually had." [3] What does it mean to feign that which it is impossible to experience? The poet "feigns" that Achilles has become angered, or that the slain Lord William has come from Paradise to return there with his bride. Is it our experience of Achilles' anger and of Lord William's "kisses cold as ice" that is "impossible"? But in a perfectly plausible sense we do experience these beings and their acts; we are made to do so. Ah, but they are not "there," they are "nowhere," and how can we experience what is nowhere? By the same equivocation, it can be proved that, regardless of the skill of the historian, there can be no experience of ancient Rome, because we can experience only the present and not the past. This piece of wisdom hinges on the decision that the term "experience" should be applied only to our relation with that which is "directly" before us in a selected framework of space and time, and not to our relation with that which is before us as communicated or depicted, as analyzed or contrived, even if the poetic traits and complexes are continuous with those encountered in non-artistic circumstances.

Does the poet "feign" in every respect? In all that he produces? Where, if at all, does his feigning end? Does he feign only places, events, and persons? Does he feign when he finds unfamiliar relations among familiar things?

> It is the sea that whitens the roof.
> The sea drifts through the winter air.
>
> It is the sea that the north wind makes.
> The sea is in the falling snow.[4]

Does the poet feign traits in the beings he recognizes as others do?

> The wind is old and still at play.[5]

Does he feign what belongs neither to fantasy nor yet to direct encounter?

> Everything that man esteems
> Endures a moment or a day:
> Love's pleasure drives his love away,
> The painter's brush consumes his dreams.[6]

We are asked by Santayana to believe that only traits present as "sensed" and not traits present as brought before us by art are constitutive of the experiencing process; that what is sensed is not comparable with what is imaged, shaped, remembered, thought, or conjectured. As if there were a danger that to acknowledge experience of the poet's creatures might make us expect to meet them on the street, or that to acknowledge experience of the traits the poet discriminates might lead us to introduce them into the sciences. Santayana ignores the multiplicity of relations and perspectives which are possible, and in effect declares them to be impossible. He ignores the forms of actuality and the forms of possibility which are subject to human encounter. If there is a problem at all in his statement of what the poet does, it lies where he least suspects it: how can that of which "an experience is impossible" be used to initiate us into "the meaning of the experience which we have actually had"?

ii

An important version of the inner-outer approach to the province of poetry is that of John Stuart Mill.[7] Mill, citing Wordsworth, says that unlike science, which "addresses itself to the belief," poetry addresses itself "to the feelings." Science tries to convince the understanding, poetry tries to move the sensibilities. In this function poetry needs to be differentiated from the novel. The novel, like poetry, seeks to act upon feeling, upon the emotions. But the emotions upon which each of the two literary forms acts are in response to what each represents and the ways in which each represents. One (the novel) represents incidents, actions, events; the other (poetry) represents feelings or emotions. The poet arouses feeling by representing feeling, the novelist arouses feeling by representing human life. Each seeks to "paint" or "portray," and to "give a true picture," but of a different aspect of human existence. The novelist represents life by describing "outward things." The poet represents "the deeper and more secret workings of the human heart"; he seeks to "paint the human soul truly." The novelist seeks knowledge of men; the

poet, knowledge of man. The novelist observes other men through
"outward experience"; the poet observes himself, and the "laws
of human emotion" revealed in himself. Poetry, or "the delinea-
tion of states of feeling," aims to portray "the inward man."

In terms of this contrast, Mill is forced to conclude that de-
scriptive, narrative, and didactic poetry are not authentic species
of poetry; or that, if they are, it is because they manage to depict
human emotion despite the bundle of irrelevances which they
bear. Mill also concludes that in the drama the representation
of incident and the representation of emotion may be, indeed
must be, combined. But he believes that "the two elements are
perfectly distinguishable." Another art from which he considers
it necessary to distinguish poetry is eloquence. Eloquence "is
heard, poetry is *overheard.*" Poetry is

feeling confessing itself to itself, in moments of solitude, and bodying
itself forth in symbols which are the nearest possible representation of
the feeling in the exact shape in which it exists in the poet's mind.

It does not, like eloquence, seek to influence action or belief. "All
poetry is of the nature of soliloquy." Although poems may be
published and circulated, "no trace of consciousness that any
eyes are upon us must be visible in the work itself."

Mill evokes from his position the general principle that poetry
"is the better part of all art whatever," and he is sure that this
principle is evident to any who find in poetry more than the im-
pression of "tickling the ear." In so far as any of the arts, paint-
ing, architecture, music, successfully "express or harmonize with"
feeling, they "partake of poetry." Mill, of course, is far from
being the only philosopher or art theorist to hold a view of this
type, though it would seem that he is partly motivated by a de-
sire to do justice to the widespread usage which applies the term
"poetic" to products of the other arts.

Mill's conception of poetry is set forth with the kind of assur-
ance and with weapons of qualification which are poised to dis-
arm criticism. If we tried to test it by selecting a variety of poems

and then asking whether each of them actually does exemplify the delineation of a state of feeling, we know what the rejoinder would be. First, that the apparent absence of direct concern with feeling in a given poem merely signifies a feeling controlled or harnessed, one made to reside in images. Or stated differently, that any other "things" poetry seems to be about are those things as composing the substance of a feeling. Second, that any function ascribed to poetry other than the portrayal of feeling is better and more fully exemplified in another discipline. But let us postpone examining the adequacy of the conception by actually confronting it with poetry, and dwell first on the meaning and consequences of the conception as such.

On the surface there seems to be a dual strain here, with respect to whether the feelings delineated are personal and unique or universal and humanly veridical. On the one hand, Mill does not emphasize that the poet expresses what he, the poet, as an individual happens to feel at a particular time. The poet looks within himself, but what he finds, or should find as an authentic poet fulfilling the office of poetry, is an emotion characteristic of or potentially belonging to all men. He paints not merely his own soul but the human soul. Though the images may be couched in personal terms, their symbolic value is paramount as a means of "painting the human soul truly." On the other hand, poetry is feeling confessing itself to itself, and the verbal symbols it employs aim to represent such feeling "in the exact shape in which it exists in the poet's mind." But the impression of duality is deceptive. To represent feeling exactly as it exists in a particular instance is the poetic way of conveying the soul, the world of feeling, truly. In accordance with this prime objective—this obligation—the soliloquizing poet moves people not by seeking to move them, for that would be eloquence and not poetry, but by representing his own emotion purely, intrinsically, and faithfully. Another way of putting Mill's point is to say that the poet's fidelity to truth is what moves others emotionally. Nor is it the fact that he paints truly, but the truth of his painting, which moves

others. The key emphasis, then, is not on the significance of idio-
syncratic feeling poetically represented, but on the truth of the
representation.

This emphasis on truth in the delineation or painting of emo-
tion naturally raises the question of how we recognize such truth.
And in the outlook of Mill this is the question of how we recog-
nize what is poetry. We do not identify a piece of literature as
poetry and then, as it were incidentally, ask whether it is true.
If poetry is not truth, it is not, in Mill's own term, "really"
poetry. A distinction would seem to be necessary between real
poetry and apparent poetry. The problem, now, of identifying or
ascertaining real poetry, poetic truth, is a crucial one. It is com-
plicated by the consideration, in Mill's approach, that the poet
does not merely convey feeling truly but above all others excels
in this function. Are we ever in a position to contradict the poet?
By the same token, are we ever in a position to commend him or
to substantiate him? We can declare him to be a non-poet, but
surely not because we, by some pre-existing standard, have su-
perior access to emotional truth. The person who essays poetry
would seem to have better title to the name of poet than one
who discovers his endeavors.

Is it the fact that we are emotionally moved which attests the
truth of the poet's work—its "real" poetic character? In what
way must we be moved? In any way? If we are outraged by the
poetry, or if it causes us to hate birds, do these reactions *ipso
facto* validate or endorse? Or is the endorsement contingent upon
the presence of another factor? Must the emotional reaction con-
tain a specific component feeling, such as the feeling of assent or
the feeling of pleasurable acceptance? But if the assent itself is
merely a feeling, a strong inclination toward approval, it can be
directed toward *any* kind of product and not be at all concerned
with truth or falsity. If the assent is provoked by a recognition
of what the poet is delineating, it is based on a sense of familiar-
ity. The spectacle of the poet arousing glad responses to familiar
and recognizable emotions is an odious one. It becomes obvious

that we cannot weigh intensity or magnitude of reaction as a criterion of truth in painting emotion, that is, as a criterion of the presence of poetry. Mill says that "if the human emotion be not painted with the most scrupulous truth, the poetry is bad poetry, i.e. is not poetry at all, but a failure." Yet, by the nature of Mill's own approach to the problem, only the poet, dedicated to the inward man, can authentically determine truth about emotion, and therefore decide whether he or any other poet is "really" a poet. What happens when poets differ in their evaluative testimony and contradict one another is distressingly unclear. The occurrence of mass favorable reaction toward a poet is inconsequential: it may be in virtue of any number of irrelevant stimuli. Nor does there seem to be room for selective critical response. However favorable this response may be, it can be based only on a more critical expression of pleasure than is ordinarily aroused, on the prediction of beneficial results, or perhaps on an expression of moral satisfaction. It cannot be based on a prior criterion of emotional truth. The poet himself does not provide a criterion; he provides the emotional truth. For the sciences, the philosopher as interpreter assumes the difficult function of defining scientific truth and defining criteria of scientific truth, even as the scientist assumes the function of providing it. But the philosopher can attempt to do this because the sciences arrive at a consensus on the issue of what, in any instance, is true or valid. The poetic critic has no analogous basis in poetry for a comparable attempt to generalize. Poets do not and cannot provide him with a history of selective validation.

Mill seems unaware of how heavily he relies on the idea of poetry as "painting." In his more conscious treatment of the relation between poetry and the other arts, he believes these arts to depend upon poetry for the full accomplishment of their purposes. Poetry, as we found him to say, "is the better part of all art whatever." It must therefore be the better part of painting. But then, can painting be the better part of poetry? That "the truth of poetry is to paint the human soul truly" depends upon the idea of true painting is clear from the fact that for Mill all literary art paints ("the truth of fiction [the novel] is to give a true picture of human *life*"). Whether the compound notion of poetry in painting and painting in poetry is a coherent one is a genuine problem. Mill gives much less attention to the way in which architecture, sculpture, and music are applicable to poetry than to the way in which poetry is applicable to them. But surely the architecture of a poem, what a poem portrays, the sculpturing of the poetic subject, and the music of a poem are concepts (or analogies) which are just as plausible as the poetry of a building, the poetry of a statue, the poetry of a portrait, and the poetry of a symphony. We need not press Mill on the problem of consistency in this area, or on the problem of felicitous analogy. It is plain that he has overreached himself. A difficult enough problem, of more immediate gravity for Mill's conception of poetry, lies in what it means to speak of "a true picture" or of "painting truly."

There are various conceptions of truth in relation to art. Some lay emphasis on the "truth of art," others on the truth of particular works of art. So far as painting goes, it is not necessary to be exercised about whether particular paintings are true. It is enough if they are good. There are also many ways of articulating their goodness. Once we grasp the extent of the difficulty in explaining what, for instance, makes Botticelli's Birth of Venus true, or Cézanne's Card Players, or Mantegna's Madonna della Vittoria—the Virgin blessing a military conqueror of the fifteenth century—wholly disregarding abstract painting, we can see that painting may be a means of understanding poetry as delineation, but not poetry as delineation of truth. Possibly attempting to rebut the tradition which sees poets as deceivers, Mill is boldly contending that the notion of truth, properly specified, actually enters into the definition of poetry. He denies the propositional character of poetic truth but supposes that he has provided for poetry an alternative conception of truth by making feeling its subject matter. That he has not provided this is indicated by our being able to ask what the distinction would be between a propositional characterization of feeling and a delineation of feeling in the poetic way. The *way* poetry delineates feeling is left unanalyzed. Even if it were analyzed, a connection would remain to be shown between the way feeling is delineated and the truth of the delineation. Some of Mill's statements suggest a view of "true" painting as duplicative reproduction, copying ("painted with the most scrupulous truth"). But in any case, such a view would not help us to understand the veracity attributed to poetry. Words cannot be used to copy in the sense that visual images (colored shapes) can. Words are not resemblances of feelings in the sense that pictures are resemblances of the pictured.

Mill had begun his analysis of poetry by asking not what poetry deals with but to what it "addresses" itself. Science presents "a proposition to the understanding," poetry does its work "by offering interesting objects of contemplation to the sensibilities." Mill thinks that he subsequently clarifies this description by specifying the "objects of contemplation" as feelings delineated. Actually the phrase taken by itself and left unspecified is more readily applicable to the diversity of practices in the history of poetry. But whatever may be the best way of saying what the work of poetry is, why must that work be addressed to the "sensibilities" or emotions? Why may it not be addressed to the "understanding"? And why may not the meaning or truth of a scientific proposition have impact on the emotions? Part of the trouble lies in the notion of "addressing." We are afraid of saying that the scientist addresses the emotions. Looked at from a different angle, the scientist and the poet do their work, they aim to validate their work in their respective ways; and the response to the work, whether of the one or the other, may be in theoretical terms, moral terms, methodological terms, practical terms, or emotional terms. Accommodating ourselves to Mill's

concepts, we can say much more on his approach than he him-
self considers permissible. For example (including some of Mill's
own assertions):

1. The propositions of science attempt to persuade the under-
   standing.
2. The delineations of poetry do not attempt persuasion of any
   kind.
3. The delineations of poetry stimulate the understanding.
4. The delineations of poetry affect and are responded to by the
   emotions.
5. The propositions of science affect and are responded to by the
   emotions.
6. The propositions of science inevitably influence belief.
7. The delineations of poetry sometimes influence belief.
8. The delineations of poetry describe emotions truly.
9. The propositions of science may describe emotions truly.

Although statement 9 would most promptly be regarded by Mill
as incompatible with his main thesis, his acceptance of it would
allow him to say that poetic soliloquy deals with emotions *more*
adequately and more extensively than science does, and with su-
perior communicative effect.

But can the secret, the deeper "workings of the human heart"
be compromised? Or the inner man? Considering the extent of
scientific findings about much that was once regarded as deep
and secret, why should the "heart" be thought inaccessible to
science and accessible to poetry? Mill's literary theory leans
heavily on the polarity of heart and head, inner and outer man.
Like many another literary theory, it is unable to resolve the
functions of literature and science, poetry and the novel. Mill has
to see the poet as soliloquizing and yet as addressing, as barely
consenting to be overheard and yet as discovering the truth about
the human soul and its laws of emotion.

Mill hovers uncertainly back and forth between the motivating emotions of the poet, the emotions the poet deals with, and the emotions the poet arouses. He takes it for granted that the motivating circumstance of poetry must be emotional, that the subject of poetry must be emotion, and that the (proper) effect of poetry must be emotional. He goes so far as to say that "the poetry of a poet is Feeling itself employing Thought only as a medium of its utterance." Accordingly, "lyric poetry" is "more eminently and peculiarly poetry than any other." That one species should be accounted a more privileged or authentic species of the genus than any other, is at least logically strange. The doctrine of the priority of "lyric" poetry is thus revealed more as the legislation of a norm than as the attempt to find a connecting link or common trait in the historical and experimental manifestations of poetry. Its legislative role does not absolve it of its theoretical failures.

That an emotion as such need not be the subject which a poem deals with is made evident by innumerable poems. Mill's protestations about the "real" subject hidden behind the putative one must be met by the truth that all subjects are real.

> The deer which lives
> On the evergreen mountain
> Where there are no autumn leaves
> Can know the coming of autumn
> Only by its own cry.[8]

In so far as feeling or emotion in *some* way is to be identified with the subject of a poem, a distinction must be made between feeling as the subject and feeling as bearing upon the subject. If we think of the latter category as the inclusive one, it can be found to take at least three forms. (1) A complex of feeling may be delineated *as* feeling. (2) A complex *other* than feeling (an everyday occurrence, the sun, the lids of Juno's eyes) may be delineated as *felt*. (3) A complex of any kind may be delineated as such—as that complex—but *in* and *through* a strong vein of feeling. Let us illustrate these three ways in which feeling may play a role, by choosing poetry not from any time and anywhere but from the work of a single poet (Keats) written a few years before the work of Mill on literary theory.

Restating (and illustrating) the three forms in which feeling bears upon the subject treated, in the first (1) a feeling *is* the dominant subject, and everything else is brought to bear to render it as it is, either in its particularity or in its generic character or in both.

> Why did I laugh to-night? No voice will tell;
>   No God, no Demon of severe response,
> Deigns to reply from Heaven or from Hell:
>   Then to my human heart I turn at once.
> Heart! Thou and I are here sad and alone;
>   I say, why did I laugh? O mortal pain!
> O Darkness! Darkness! ever must I moan,
>   To question Heaven and Hell and Heart in vain.
> Why did I laugh? I know this Being's lease,
>   My fancy to its utmost blisses spreads;
> Yet would I on this very midnight cease,
>   And the world's gaudy ensigns see in shreds;
> Verse, Fame, and Beauty are intense indeed,
>   But Death intenser—Death is Life's high meed.[9]

In the second form, (2), the subject is not a complex which constitutes a feeling, but a complex which is transmuted by the feeling of it. Thus Keats's goddess Psyche is the subject whose domain ("temple thou hast none") the poet seeks to define. It gets defined by the directions which his passion takes.

> Yes, I will be thy priest, and build a fane
>   In some untrodden region of my mind,
> Where branched thoughts, new-grown with pleasant pain,
>   Instead of pines shall murmur in the wind:
> Far, far around shall those dark-cluster'd trees
>   Fledge the wild-ridged mountains steep by steep;
> And there by zephyrs, streams, and birds, and bees,
>   The moss-lain Dryads shall be lulled to sleep,
> And in the midst of this wide quietness

A rosy sanctuary will I dress
With the wreath'd trellis of a working brain,
 With buds, and bells, and stars without a name,
With all the gardener Fancy e'er could feign,
 Who breeding flowers, will never breed the same:
And there shall be for thee all soft delight
 That shadowy thought can win,
A bright torch, and a casement ope at night,
 To let the warm Love in! [10]

In the third form, (3), a complex is dealt with as possessing the character that it has, quite apart from feeling; but the emphasis on its (independent) integrity is achieved by *means* of intensified feeling.

I cannot see what flowers are at my feet,
 Nor what soft incense hangs upon the boughs,
But, in embalmed darkness, guess each sweet
 Wherewith the seasonable month endows
The grass, the thicket, and the fruit-tree wild;
 White hawthorn, and the pastoral eglantine;
 Fast fading violets cover'd up in leaves;
  And mid-May's eldest child,
The coming musk-rose, full of dewy wine,
 The murmurous haunt of flies on summer eves.[11]

The appeal to the inner does not shed light on the traits of poetry. There is no doubt that various meanings for "inner" can be enunciated, and that all of them can be made tenable within a narrow metaphysical range. But to speak of what is "in" a poet's *world* or in any man's world must be done with care; it cannot be done in traditional philosophic terms, and it cannot be improvised with common sense notions. The poet has no need to retreat to the arcane or to pull rabbits from a hat. The inward man is one who at best is self-critical or self-explorative. No one believes any longer that the self is bounded by the skull or the skin, yet it remains hard for many to say that the self is relational, or that it is indefinite in its scope. The domain of self, "in" which so much can be found, overlaps with other domains or perspectives, some of them selves and others relevant to selves—all of them human orders of life and production. It overlaps just as pervasively with non-human orders of being. The exploration of a self is the exploration of the world in so far as the world is relevant to a man as that man; relevant to the actualities and possibilities of his life. To say, therefore, that a man may turn to self or away from self refers to different or conflicting interests and concerns; it does not refer to disparate worlds or mutually exclusive realms. The so-called private world or private worlds are those perspectives (human orders) which are assumed to overlap with no other. But a private perspective is marked by traits continuous with the traits of other private perspectives and public perspectives—temporality, spatiality, language, emotion . . . there is no end of these. Otherwise stated, the private order overlaps with the orders of space, time, language, emotion . . . Its character is ascertainable from the kind of orders it excludes, not from the exclusion of all other orders. What is important to the poet as poet is not the privacies of his existence but the worth of his production. What is "in" the life and world of any human consists largely of what he has the power to do and has done, the power to say and has said, the power to make and has made. For the poet, no other "in" is necessary. Paraphrasing Locke, to say that an idea—a discriminandum of any kind—is "in the understanding" is to say no more than that it is discriminated. Not the inner world of the poet but the nature of poetic discrimination is what we need to grasp.

iii

Somewhat akin (as we shall find) to the view of poetry as delineation of feeling is the view (here represented in the version of Max Eastman) that poetry aims "to convey the quality of an experience," or that poetry is "a communication of the qualities of things."[12] The "experience" is construed as the experience *of* "things," whether these are poetically dealt with as present to perceptual encounter or as present to awareness of some other kind. The consciousness regarded as antithetical to poetic consciousness is that of practicality, of the uses of things. Poetry's words suggest "impractical identifications." (Eastman overstates the thesis when he also says, conversely, "any impractical identification that you can induce somebody to listen to is poetic, because it is the essence of an attentive consciousness." This last little qualification of the theory may be dismissed quickly. There are many ways of listening and many purposes for which listening takes place. Men listen with attentive consciousness for scientific and philosophic purposes as well as for the sound and "qualities" conveyed by words. But with respect to the larger point, scientific and philosophic identifications are ordinarily as impractical as those of poetry, at least as soon as we are able to see that science is more than technology, and philosophy more than prudential wisdom. To suggest that "prosaic" and "practical" are synonymous, as Eastman does, is to suggest a clear falsehood. And of course the narrative prose of a novel may also be as impractical as the theoretic prose of science.)

The emphasis on poetry as conveying the qualities of what we experience is accompanied by an equal emphasis on poetry as "the attempt to make words suggest the given-in-experience." Whether it is "qualities" which *are* "the given-in-experience" thus becomes a central question. When poetry achieves this function (or these functions) it produces a "heightened consciousness" (the phrase ascribed to Edith Sitwell). The thesis of Eastman is basically shared by F. A. Pottle, but with an important modification, namely, that "the heightened consciousness which is the mark of poetry may result either from an awareness of individual concrete objects or of generalized objects. Whether it results from one or the other will depend upon the basis of sensibility. One can have a consciousness of Man as well as of a man; of 'leaden death' as well as of a bullet." [13]

In examining the theory, we find at once that the meaning of "quality" is crucial. Typically we should say that there are many kinds of qualities that "things" have. There are, for example, physical, optical, geometrical, and physiological qualities. These are not the kinds of qualities cited when reference is made to qualities "given-in-experience." The qualities favored for this purpose are described as "sense" qualities: visual, tactile, olfactory, for example. Some qualities may be said to be "experienced" not through the everyday senses but through inquiry. It is obvious that, depending upon the scope and nature we assign to what we call "qualities," the function of conveying qualities may be very broad or very narrow. Even if we restrict the range of qualities to the familiar kinds, say qualities of human character like decency, fairness, persistence, disloyalty, and unreliability, these seem far more ramified and extensive than the qualities which are held to be "given-in-experience." Of course, if "given-in-experience" meant "available to experience," and if "experience" carried the import of "human experience," we should be able to include far more than we do when we mean what empiricist philosophers usually have meant, namely, "immediately given" or "presented as uninterpreted."

Suppose, when it is said that poetry conveys qualities, it is indeed the qualities of "things" that are intended, and not qualities of "immediate experience." The latter, in any case, could only in a very difficult respect be conveyed as immediate when they are mediated, shaped, and colored by poetic language. A knock on the head or a punch in the nose would do better than poetry toward the unworthy end of merely conveying immediacy, and would do as well in the heightening or lowering of consciousness. But if it is any quality at all that poetry may convey, we must decide with what scope we are using the term "quality," or at least what scope we intend to give it. Some people, including some philosophers, make the word synonymous with "trait." But if by a quality we intended any sort of trait, then we would have to acknowledge that science and philosophy convey the qualities of things no less than poetry. We should then have to say more about conveying—what kind of conveying, in what way qualities are conveyed. It would not be enough to add that a certain kind of effect is produced by poetry, namely, heightened consciousness; for philosophy and science can be said to heighten consciousness in one way or another, if we wished to speak this way at all. But the problem is not yet ended, when we equate quality with trait. For if we then insist on defining poetry as the discipline which conveys qualities experienced, are we not making the domain of poetry co-extensive with all other domains? Philosophy and science also convey traits that are experienced. They are experienced in a different way, or more accurately, in various other ways. The same difficulty arises if we hold, as Lascelles Abercrombie does, that "poetry is the translation of experience into language." [14] Philosophy, science, and religion all translate experience into language—*their* experience, their mode and level of experience, their complexes experienced. As we have seen in another context, poetry cannot be described intelligibly as the domain of "experience." At best, it would have to be a domain characterized by a certain kind of experience. What we should have to say is that whatever traits are experienced by any discipline can also be experienced poetically, experienced by poetry in its own way. And the question once again becomes, In what way? How are qualities conveyed poetically? The definition offered begs the fundamental question.

Many who speak of "qualities experienced" do not at all mean to equate quality and trait. And actually they do not mean to talk of qualities experienced, but of qualities *felt*, that is, if we prefer, qualities "experienced" in a relatively narrow sense of the term. But then, we are prompted to ask which qualities are those capable of being felt. The answer may turn out to be that, whichever qualities *can* be said to be felt are those which poetry conveys, however many or few these may be. But we do not escape the question, Conveyed in what way? For many people who are far from being poets convey the qualities they feel. They communicate them in speech or otherwise, and in some cases they

even "heighten consciousness" in a most spectacular if vulgar
way.

We deserve to know more fully what is to be understood by
a "quality" if we are to understand what is intended and what
excluded by the view that poetry conveys the quality of what is
experienced. If qualities are not the only traits there are, what
kinds of traits are *not* conveyed by poetry? Structures? Rela-
tions? Potentialities? Do we experience structures and relations?
Surely in some sense we do. Why then does poetry not convey
the structure of what we experience; why only the quality? There
would seem to be but one way to recover the original thesis, a
way to which we have already been driven though less forcefully,
and which at the same time helps to explain why an emphasis on
the "given-in-experience" is joined with the emphasis on the
communication of quality. This way is to assume that in a posi-
tion like Eastman's, "quality" tacitly *means* "feeling." The posi-
tion would be that poetry conveys the feeling which things
arouse in us, and that this cannot be said of any other discipline.
We are now back essentially to the definition of poetry given by
Mill. Whether Mill would have wished to acknowledge the
"things"; whether Eastman would have wished to acknowledge
the "delineation" is of course problematical. But "things" is
vague enough for anyone to acknowledge. And if the poet is to
convey feeling uniquely, he cannot do so by simply *causing* it in
others.

iv

Whitehead (regarded by Eastman as one of the philosophers who
have been "waking up" to "the real nature of poetry") once said,
"I hold that the ultimate appeal is to naïve experience and that is
why I lay such stress on the evidence of poetry." [15] The implica-
tion appears to be either that poetry conveys naïve experience or
that poetry draws upon naïve experience for the essential charac-
ter of the knowledge and meaning it conveys. If the expression

"naïve experience" were all we had to rely upon to make the position intelligible, it would be futile to go much farther. The scope of this notion is simply too unclear. In the immediate context, however, Whitehead seems to identify "naïve experience" with "sense-experience." It is in knowledge that Whitehead is here interested: "ultimate appeal" refers to a final arbiter which either grounds or contravenes what men propose as knowledge. This is not the place to examine fully the merit of the claim as Whitehead states it, or to evaluate its unrestricted formulation. What it is important to see is that we are not helped very much more by "sense-experience" than by "naïve experience," particularly so far as poetry is concerned.

It is not easy to discover here whether "sense" is intended to refer, as it does traditionally and loosely, to familiar, everyday aspects of encounter (the "five" senses), or intended to apply much more widely. That the term "perception" and the term "feeling" should refer to far more than they do in familiar speech is basic to Whitehead's thought. He declares "non-sensuous" perception to be as fundamental as "sensuous" perception. Non-sensuous perception is illustrated by the perception of "our own immediate past" [16] or of "passing from oneself in the present towards oneself in the future." [17] Yet we find Whitehead speaking also of *this* kind of perception in terms of *sense:* "a sense of influx of influences," "a sense of derivation from an immediate past," a "sense of existence." Apparently "non-sensuous" perception is sensuous in *some* undisclosed way. Whether Whitehead, in proclaiming what the "ultimate appeal" is, allows us to include such sensings as these in the scope of "sense-experience"; whether he would also include, for example, a sense of disquiet or a sense of well-being along with the sense of sound or color, is uncertain. When sense and sense-experience are commonly spoken of, when it is "the senses" that are intended however vaguely, the tacit reference is to familiar types of felt qualities, to a group chosen over and over again. These qualities reflect a correlation of a particular sense mode with an organ or

a function of the body. On what basis should it be decided
whether or not all of the various sensings mentioned exemplify
a "bodily" function? Is a line to be drawn between bodily sens-
ing and the kind expressed, say, by "sensing the drift of what
you are saying"? It is clear enough that the kind of relation said
to obtain between poetry and sense experience will vary signifi-
cantly with the ways in which the scope of "sense" can be speci-
fied.

With respect to his "ultimate appeal," Whitehead fails also
to distinguish between sense-experience as inevitably *present* in
the process of validation and sense-experience as that which vali-
dates. By way of example, suppose we aim to know whether a
personal acquaintance is trustworthy. We cannot avoid sense-
experience in the process of deciding, but it may well be that
no sensed object or sensory situation can be the deciding factor.
The decision may come from (the "appeal" may be to) accumu-
lated knowledge of a structure of relations which is not available
sensuously. Or suppose a painter to be unsure whether he knows
what is the best hue for the body of St. Sebastian. The fact that
he is practically enmeshed in sense-experience, and that it is a
sensory vehicle which he is seeking, may be quite insufficient for
the resolution of his perplexity. No amount of color and no di-
versity of shape may be able to settle this question. Other, non-
sensory considerations (say of a religious or moral kind) may
predominate and determine the appropriateness of his final sen-
sory choice, which would thereby serve as a means to an end.
It seems clear that in poetry the use of "sensory" devices of lan-
guage does not necessarily limit the poet to "sense"-experience
as his domain of exploration and as the burden of his communi-
cation.

We cannot begin to understand, then, what is "the evidence of
poetry" without (as a beginning) understanding what is intended
by "sense-experience" or "naïve experience." But why, in any
case, poetry and a strictly *limited* phase of experience should be
so fundamentally connected, is puzzling. What reason have we to

believe that poetry arises chiefly out of sense-experience or that it necessarily derives its intelligibility from sense-experience? Drawing upon the poetry that Whitehead himself chooses for the purpose of defining the trends of modern thought, consider these lines from Milton's *Paradise Lost* (I, 17–26), of which Whitehead quotes the last three:

> And chiefly thou, O Spirit, that dost prefer
> Before all temples th' upright heart and pure,
> Instruct me, for thou know'st; thou from the first
> Wast present, and with mighty wings outspread,
> Dove-like sat'st brooding on the vast abyss,
> And mad'st it pregnant: what in me is dark
> Illumine, what is low raise and support;
> That, to the height of this great argument,
> I may assert Eternal Providence,
> And justify the ways of God to men.

The sensory images here are essential in the constitution of what is set forth, but the dominant meaning and stress cannot be said to be either reduced to them or derived from them. Sense-experience here, in other words, is utilized in conjunction with Scriptural and ethical inspiration, to help build the structure; but it is not what we should wholly or even mainly rely upon if we sought to grasp the direction which the poem is taking. An analogous outcome obtains with respect to the lines quoted by Whitehead from the opening of Pope's *Essay on Man*:

> Awake, my St. John! leave all meaner things
> To low ambition, and the pride of kings.
> Let us (since life can little more supply
> Than just to look about us and to die)
> Expatiate free o'er all this scene of man;
> A mighty maze! but not without a plan.

The question whether sensory images are necessarily present in poetry, like the question whether they are the only kind of image in poetry, once again awaits a clarification of "sensory." It can

be as difficult to hold that some poetic images are not sensory as
to prove that all are. A coupling of sensory images, each of the
most familiar mode, may add up to a compound that can scarcely
be called either sensory or naïve experience:

No hungry generations tread thee down.[18]

One conception of non-sensory images, as structural resem-
blances or parallels, is widely held. But it is not easy to apply.
A view discussed by Hooker regards the Law as an image of the
wisdom of God. Georg Simmel thinks of each system of philos-
ophy as providing an image of the world. The Whiteheadian po-
sition would seem to be that in poetry sensory images are crucial,
inevitable, and central. This position can be pursued stubbornly,
even in the face of a view like Rimbaud's that the poet must
struggle to "see" not the familiar but the "unknown" and the
"invisible," and that he cannot do so except by a "rational dis-
ordering of all the senses." [19] The reason the position can be pur-
sued is that for Whitehead (and Locke) the sensory elements re-
main constant and would be recognizable within the disorder.
The disorganization of the sensory patterns cannot be a destruc-
tion of their defining *components*, and the purpose of the dis-
organization can only be to achieve novel organization among
these components. To Whitehead, the sensory components are
universal characters: these cannot be destroyed but only embod-
ied uniquely, represented anew, in individual occasions.

Some philosophers have suggested that "naïve experience" or
"primary experience" (Dewey) is the experience of the most re-
current and most insistent traits in the environment of men. It
comprises the rough, inevitable, gross identifications. Any disci-
pline, in their view, cannot do other than "appeal" for support
to so reliable and so pervasive a dimension of experience—to a
fund that is always "there." And any discipline does this, no
doubt, if it is a certain type of inquiry that needs a resource of

reliable confirming conditions. But to suppose that poetry exemplifies such a discipline is to make a mockery of the art. It is the last possible domain in which we would seek to preserve by language what we commonly deem to be reliable cognitive commonplaces, and the last to appeal to solid, everyday perceptions. Poetry does not seek to negate these props. But it uncovers the oppressions of naïve experience and the stale pool of confirming constancies.

III
THE IDEA OF
CONCRETENESS

i

When poetry is conceded to have a concern with the world and not merely the "inner" world, and with natural complexes besides feeling, we are in a position to ask, What kind of concern is it? To what is it directed? What form does it take? According to a widely held position which provides answers to these questions, the key to poetry is Concreteness. This position seems to have benefited the morale of theorists who feel themselves primarily obliged to justify poetry as cognitively valuable, as contributing knowledge of "reality." It is a position which attributes to poetry a specific angle of interest in the world, and which believes it has found a convincing difference between poetic and non-poetic language. Let us start with two versions of the Concreteness thesis.

According to Philip Wheelwright,

The first and most indispensable attribute of poetic language is its radical particularity of reference, its presentative immediacy. . . . it presents as well as represents, it evokes something of the very quality, tone and flavor of the concrete *qua* concrete with a directness and a full experiential relevance that [non-poetic] symbols cannot do.

Underlying this function of poetry is the metaphysical truth that

What is directly confronted in experience is always, in its first phase, something individual. When you pass from generalizations about mankind to direct acquaintance with Bill Smith, and with some particular grief or enthusiasm that Bill Smith is undergoing, you pass from concepts to real existence.

And "poetic language undertakes to speak of the concrete particulars with directness and experiential precision." No scientific definition or analysis can give us the "full living actuality" of, say, a flower, "as adequately" as poetry can.[1]

We are told by Samuel Alexander that poetry, in comparison with prose,

is the higher art because of its distinguishingly concrete character, which takes it nearer to the nature of things.

(Whitehead, too, names "poetry" and "drama" as literature "in its more concrete forms.") Poetry aspires "to make the subject a concrete and living thing." In a poem

the subject as rendered in words . . . acquires a life of its own, is a living thing, as it were, living its own life like an animal or plant, is organic, and, in a word, concrete.

Prose, by contrast, is "analytic." The poet

places himself and places his hearer within the subject itself, and works from within outwards, while the prosaist describes, relatively, from without.

And "analysis is nearer to reflection, poetry is nearer to the simpler, directer, experience of things."[2]

Now in order to discuss the merit of these two positions on the matter of concreteness, it is necessary to find out something more about what they imply. The questions we need to ask are not, as it happens, either answered or obviated by the larger contexts in

which the positions are located. First of all, how should we go
about understanding "concreteness"? What is it that should be
called "concrete"? Is Bill Smith concrete? But even as this question
is being asked, the preceding question re-imposes itself upon us:
just what is it that we are trying to identify? A particular body
in space and time? A body here, now, in the span of present per-
ceptual attention? A being simply called by the name Bill Smith?
The man who has many fears and whose life is directed more
consciously to the future than to the present or the past? The
red-headed occupant of the next house? Is each of these con-
crete? Or is each of these only an "abstraction" from the concrete
Bill Smith who is all of these rolled into one? Which is "real ex-
istence," the various parts and components of Bill Smith, or cer-
tain of these, or Bill Smith as a "whole"—the natural complex
of emotions, opinions, spatial positions, and relations that con-
stitute the man of this name? When we are said to "confront"
this Bill Smith, "something individual," is it the name "Bill
Smith" or the body Bill Smith or the complex whole Bill Smith
or the image Bill Smith? Which is the "individual" that we "di-
rectly confront in experience"? Some poets who choose to deal
with a Bill Smith (Agamemnon, John Brown, Hamlet) treat his
history or a large portion of it as of equal importance with any
given constituent of that history, any event or trait within it.

If we ask whether Agamemnon, Circe, and the Trojan Horse
are concrete particulars, the answer may be, No, but they are
treated by the poet as if they were; he evokes the quality of con-
creteness in them. If so, then would the poet be conveying the
concreteness of subjects that are not "real existences"? May
concreteness be found and evoked in anything, whether that in
which it is found is particular or not? But we still do not know
what is being evoked. We do not know in what concreteness
consists, or what exemplifies it. May anything be treated as an
individual? Is a war an individual—an individual war? Is the
Trojan War an individual? Is the Trojan *War* evoked as concrete,
or only a number of incidents and participants in that war? Is the

decline of a culture an individual? Is it a concrete particular? Is it dealt with poetically as if it *were* a concrete particular, or is it dealt with by *means* of concrete particulars? But as we continue to see, it is uncertain *what* it is by means of which anything is thus to be dealt with. Are possibilities ever concrete, or only actualities? After all, there are possibilities of a general nature (e.g. the possibility of life somewhere else in the astronomical universe) and possibilities of a specific or localized nature (e.g. the possibility that I will run out of writing paper before next Monday). "Real existence," designed to mark out the area of what is concrete, is a crude, vague shibboleth. That we can "confront" possibilities *as* possibilities, just as plainly as we confront actualities, should by itself cause some doubt about many commonly cherished metaphysical assumptions, especially when a domain like poetry is being analyzed on their basis. A merchant confronts the possibility of becoming bankrupt no less than he confronts the actuality of the bills on his desk. We may accept a counter-protest that possibilities cannot be regarded as separable from actualities, provided we add that neither can actualities be regarded as separable from possibilities. What partly distinguishes one actuality from another is the difference in its possibilities—the possibilities belonging to *it*. But although the possible and the actual cannot be regarded as separable from one another, possibilities can be regarded *as* possibilities, and encountered *as* such; and actualities can be regarded *as* actualities, and encountered *as* such.

If actualities alone are to be called "concrete," what *kind* of actualities? Actual individuals (a complicated enough notion) are not separable from relations which obtain among their constituents or from relations which obtain between them and other individuals that enter into their being—that in part determine them as the individuals they are. Poets seize and embody all these orders of what is. The deficiencies lie in the theory of poetry, which has failed to articulate theoretically what poets have articulated poetically. Poets deal with possibilities as well

as actualities, with cultures as well as persons, with structures
as well as moments and situations, with relations as well as indi-
viduals, with concepts as well as particulars, with the ugly as
well as the beautiful, with moral traits as well as sheer occur-
rences, with the constant and the evanescent, the recurrent and
the unique, the historical and the atemporal, with particular
primroses and with flowers as flowers—with any natural com-
plex whatever. And there is no reason to believe, either from
a historical examination of poetry or from an analysis of its
functions and practices, that any of these types of complex is
the one into which all the others are sought to be transformed,
or is the one into which all the others as types of subjects are
meant to be expressed. *How* poetry deals with any complex, and
what warrants the use of the term "poetic" is the problem at
issue.

The ideas of "concreteness," "presentative immediacy," "rad-
ical particularity of reference," and the like cannot be allowed
to rest here; they need further examination. But we also should
question their practical application, even when they are thought
of in a rough intuitive way. Are these "indispensable attributes
of poetic language" present in the following lines?

    It seems, as one becomes older,
That the past has another pattern, and ceases to be a mere sequence—
Or even development: the latter a partial fallacy,
Encouraged by superficial notions of evolution,
Which becomes, in the popular mind, a means of disowning the past.
The moments of happiness—not the sense of well-being,
Fruition, fulfilment, security or affection,
Or even a very good dinner, but the sudden illumination—
We had the experience but missed the meaning,
And approach to the meaning restores the experience
In a different form, beyond any meaning
We can assign to happiness. I have said before
That the past experience revived in the meaning
Is not the experience of one life only
But of many generations—not forgetting

Something that is probably quite ineffable:
The backward look behind the assurance
Of recorded history, the backward half-look
Over the shoulder, towards the primitive terror.
Now, we come to discover that the moments of agony
(Whether, or not, due to misunderstanding,
Having hoped for the wrong things or dreaded the wrong things,
Is not in question) are likewise permanent
With such permanence as time has. We appreciate this better
In the agony of others, nearly experienced,
Involving ourselves, than in our own.
For our own past is covered by the currents of action,
But the torment of others remains an experience
Unqualified, unworn by subsequent attrition.
People change, and smile: but the agony abides.[3]

"What is directly confronted in experience is always, in its first phase, something individual." How are we to understand "first phase" and "directly confronted"? Presumably we are not concerned with what is genetically first in a man's life; but it is relevant to observe, as Aristotle did, that the earliest identifications made by a child are broad identifications, recognitions not sharply bounded. The child does not begin by selecting "individuals" whom it later relates to other individuals that have been independently defined, but achieves its desired recognitions by an increasingly critical process. Individuals come to be differentiated; they are not the irreducible basis of differentiation but emerge in awareness out of a "grey chaotic indiscriminateness" (William James).

If it is not this first phase in development but rather the first phase of a given situation that we are talking about, can we say that what is "directly confronted" is always the confrontation of an "individual"? Most philosophers assume that individuals are the prototype of being. They are the "real existences" which as it were underlie or carry all other aspects of being. They alone are visible, and all else is inferred, or found lurking here and there, around, between, behind them. The structural, the

relational, the temporal and spatial are deemed at best modifica-
tions of individuals—assuming that these modifications are rec-
ognized as "real" in even a secondary sense. This encourages
the belief that individuals are absolutely determinate; that any
individual "entity" is, as Whitehead thinks, "all or none" (even
though it is complex and analyzable). In this dogma Whitehead
and Aristotle and most traditions of metaphysical theory are in
agreement. For, they ask in effect, is it not the case that in what-
ever happens and in all that there is, there must always be a
"this," an individual "thing" *to* which it happens and which *is*
related and structured, which *has* the possibilities and *bears* all
other traits? But the dogma is double-barrelled. If there cannot
be structures without individuals which are structured, neither
can there be individuals without a structure that constitutes
them the individuals they are. If there are no relations except
among individuals, neither are there individuals which are un-
related. If there would be no possibilities unless they belonged
to individuals, neither would there be individuals unless there
were possibilities which they actualized or embodied. Any claim
of ontological priority, which the conception of the individual
as the "primary reality" illustrates, can be shown, in consequence
of the paradoxes which it engenders, to yield to a principle of
ontological parity. Complexes independent or dependent, im-
portant or unimportant, of cause or effect, organic or inorganic,
are all realities; though not all are the *kind* of reality we may be
interested in, and not all are relevant to a specific purpose of
emphasis, say moral, military, or psychiatric. We shall see that,
so far as the poet's product as poetic product is concerned, a
doctrine of ontological priority is alien. The multiplicity of com-
plexes that he is able to grant recognition to, the kinds of dif-
ferences and similarities that he discloses, cannot be obliterated
or declared illusory, and cannot be declared to be either more or
less "real" than any other. Implicitly, in the history and variety
of his work through the ages, he may be said to be the chief ex-
emplar of the principle of ontological parity.

We have met an increasing number of obstacles to our discerning a defensible position in statements like Alexander's "[poetry] is the higher art because of its distinguishingly concrete character, which takes it nearer to the *nature of things*" (italics added). (Pending later consideration, we may also recall Alexander's statement that "poetry is nearer to the simpler, directer experience of things." A close connection seems to be implied between "the nature of things" and "the simpler, directer experience of things.") Now there are many contexts in which reference to "the nature of things" is significant. The phrase is almost always loose and colloquial, yet not useless; the rhetoric of fundamental issues requires some kind of general allusion to traits and patterns not of our making or beyond our present ken. In a similar vein, we speak of "the powers that be" or of what lies "in the lap of the gods." But the context before us is an entirely different matter. It is one in which the phrase purports to clarify and define. One can only marvel at the assessment of relative *distances* from "the nature of things." One is constrained to ask whether, in this phrase, the emphasis is on "things" or on "nature." If the emphasis is on "things," should we not know what is the purview of "thing"? If the emphasis is on "nature," what is the *status* of that which is far from it? Is that which is farther from it not itself some kind of "thing"? Does it not have a "nature" of its own? What are the marks of that which is closer? Are living things the things that are closer —"more real"? Non-living things, then, must be "less" real. A dying thing, we must infer, is becoming less and less real all the time. But then living things must be getting less and less real all the time, since they are coming closer and closer to death. Is dying not concrete—at least to the dying? Among temporarily living things like human beings, which of them are nearer to the nature of things? Would it be the man who scorns all abstractions in favor of "concrete realities"? The "man of action," who gets nearer to things by taking matters into his own hands? The man who condemns as "unnatural" what is uncongenial to him? If the poet as poet is close to "the nature of things," he is at least very far from these attitudes. Is he closer to or farther from nature than the scientist? The covert, inevitably self-contradictory assumption in any conception of "nearness to nature" is that we already know more about what we are trying to get near to than any of the disciplines by which we can possibly hope to understand it.

The vague reference to "things" is not rare; it is distressingly common among philosophers. Santayana says we must concede that "poetic notions are false notions," for they contain "elements not present in things." [4] Not present in things of *any* kind? If so, then many complexes discriminated by the poet and present to his awareness are being dismissed absolutely from all possible worlds—a contradiction if ever there was one. If "things" means, more narrowly, "what is physical," the arbitrary verdict involved should be made clear. That even a brilliant writer should be so inarticulate as to appeal philosophically to "things" in interpreting the nature of poetic products stems from a metaphysical failure. Santayana is afraid that conceding the poet's chosen world to be "real" leaves the door open to the justification of all claims. But a recognition of what the poet has discriminated, of the complexes he has shaped, does not imply that he is making a claim, nor does it imply that any cognitive value attributed to his poetry demeans other forms of knowledge.

Dropping now absurd phrases like "nearer to the nature of things" and "present in things," let us ask why poetry should be held to be "concrete" and the novel not. Does the novel not aim "to make the subject a concrete and living thing"? Does it deal with beings who are depicted as living but who are not alive? Should the stress be that poetry can *make* the subject "a concrete and living thing," and the novel cannot? (One difference between Wheelwright and Alexander seems to be that the former, for the most part, conceives of poetry as conveying the sense of what is concrete in a subject; the latter, for the most part, conceives of poetry as making a subject concrete.) And why, or in virtue of what attributes, is this accomplished by poems and not by novels? The only clue we are given to an answer is that in poetry the subject is treated as "organic" and in prose the subject is treated "analytically." Even assuming that what is intended by these concepts or by the use of these concepts is clear, it would be reasonable to ask why poetry cannot be said to "analyze" its subject in a manner appropriate to it; why prose cannot be said to deal with its subject as "organic"; or why poetry and prose cannot each be said to deal with their subjects in both ways or in either way, depending on the purpose at hand. The further answer of Alexander seems to be that the poet places himself "within" the subject and works "outwards" while the novelist "describes, relatively, from without." Again we can pursue the same kinds of questions and receive the same kinds of answers or none at all. For we are among sacred cows—"concrete," "organic," "inside the subject," "outside the subject"—to which deference has been given uncritically. In the final chapter we shall focus on the idea of "analysis," for the purpose of showing how loosely treated a notion it has been philosophically despite the frequency of its use. We shall try to show how it may be interpreted both less narrowly and more clearly, and in what sense it characterizes poetry.

The living, the organic, and the concrete are treated in the context of Alexander as if, by constant conjunction, they explained one another, so that we end up with a sort of compound slogan continually rephrased, the lame the halt and the blind stumbling along in a fruitless circle. If the term "living" were construed in the biological sense and opposed to the "non-living," the contrast made between poetry and the novel would be plainly false. No novel can be said to be a novel without primary attention to living beings affecting and affected by a world, whereas there is poetry which either does not deal or deals only in segments with living creatures or with persons as the subjects of principal concern.

> The atoms, as their own weight bears them down
> Plumb through the void, at scarce determined times,
> In scarce determined places, from their course
> Decline a little—call it, so to speak,
> Mere changèd trend. For were it not their wont
> Thuswise to swerve, down would they fall, each one,
> Like drops of rain, through the unbottomed void;
> And then collisions ne'er could be nor blows
> Among the primal elements; and thus
> Nature would never have created aught.[5]

Poetry, we are told, *treats* the subject as organic, *makes* it a living thing. Yet when we attempt to discover, organic in what sense, living in what sense, we find the thesis to be no more enlightening than its converse: to say that a subject is treated organically, made a living thing, means that it is treated *poetically*. Nor would it help, in explaining what is meant, to speak of poetry "making the subject come alive." Any significant undertaking, any linguistic discipline worth its salt, makes its subject "come alive."

What about the "full living actuality" (Wheelwright) which poetry is said to convey to us and which no scientific definition or analysis is held able to match? It is good to think of poetry as capable of concern with actuality, with actual goings-on, and not merely (as so many have said) with pleasurable fabrications. The confusion threatened on this point, as we have already suggested, derives from an assumption that what is not actual can only be what is "fictitious." This reduces *possibility* to the fictitious and therefore to a secondary ontological status. Usually, little time is spent clarifying the meaning of "fiction"; much more is spent debating its relation to "reality." But turning attention now to "full living actuality"—a measuring contest apparently is in order, to determine how full a description can be, to ascertain the greatest degree of vividness. Which wins the contest, a scientific account or a poetic account? Let each side choose its favorite subject, and then tackle that subject. If we shrink from such a formidable task of assessment, perhaps we should compare the vividness of the subjects likely to be chosen. In the best conservative tradition, we wager on a tie. But if compelled to choose, we in this corner are willing to give the nod to science. Can the vividness of any poem exceed that of a detailed medical report on the symptoms of a tropical disease? or the description of a body maimed in war? or the chilling completeness of the diagnosis of a plague? or the psychiatric account of a knife-wielding paranoiac? . . . Abandoning this entire quixotic enterprise of comparison, we observe the uncertain and arid ground to which we can be pushed by eulogism and uncritical metaphysics. To say that poetry alone conveys "full" living actuality does not illuminate the nature of poetry, and whatever sense it makes shows it to be false.

Consider the view of Wheelwright that "the first and most indispensable attribute of poetic language is its radical particularity of reference, its presentative immediacy." It is important to note that among philosophers "presentative immediacy" is as likely to be opposed to "particularity of reference" as to be identified with it. What is involved in such immediacy has been construed, for example, as, not an encounter with particularity but an encounter with the common or universal elements of perception; with the sensory data which are exemplified and repeated in innumerable perceptual situations. And according to another viewpoint, that aspect of a perceptual situation—of any human situation—known as immediacy, its unmediated or uninterpreted state, is its mute, inarticulate, indeterminate aspect; in immediacy, neither particularity nor universality manifests itself. But whatever may be true of immediacy *per se*, immediacy gets to be mediated in so far as it is humanly appropriated. And as immediacy turns into mediated awareness, it can evoke in us a sense of the particular *or* a sense of the universal, a sense of the peculiar or a sense of the common, a sense of the unique or a sense of the regular, a sense of difference or a sense of sameness, and most basically, a sense of the actual or a sense of the possible. In any of our experiences, whether or not it has the character of "immediacy," we can encounter what *is* actual or what *is* possible, what has come about or what may come of it. If "presentative immediacy" is taken to be indispensable to poetic language, it is clear that the communication of particularity is not necessarily implied. Every actuality and every possibility is located in a complex of actualities and possibilities. In one sense, what we always encounter is an interpretable natural complex. What philosophers unfortunately have called "the given in experience" is not only never simple or pure; it is not any one kind of natural complex. Yet in another and perfectly compatible sense, our encounter is selectively directed to this or that constituent of the complex—this or that aspect of its actuality, this or that aspect of its possibilities. In our encounters we are influenced by what has been and what can be. The complex encountered *may* take the form, may assume the role, of a particularity. Poetic language *may* entail a "radical particularity of reference"—it also may *not*.

The idea of Alexander that "poetry is nearer to the simpler, directer experience of things" whereas prose, implying "analysis," is "nearer to reflection," is exposed now in its utter weakness. If poetry ever excelled in bold inventiveness, it is through appropriation by language of the most recalcitrant of complexes, which include those most taken for granted. Poetry in practice is as effective a refutation of the "simple, direct experience" thesis as any philosophic argument could be. Like philosophy, science, and all inventive disciplines, it discriminates the unsuspected in what passes as commonplace. Whether it should be called "reflection" or not is relatively unimportant. It is methodic, and inventively methodic.[6] It cannot be restricted a priori in the character or range of its subjects. In *its* way it converts the opaque into the accessible. It is neither "near" nor "far" from the "simple." Ironically, the critical attention given to poetic "indirection," to the so-called *indirect* character of its linguistic devices, is considerable.

The notions of linguistic directness and indirectness are difficult. However they are to be analyzed, it would seem that they must be linked to strategies and circumstances in language. To think of poetic language as *either* direct *or* indirect is to approach it by the standards of everydayness and horse sense, by the irrelevant (though in themselves often useful) standards of gross identification. Once again, we are forced to ask where the emphasis lies in the phrase "simpler, directer experience of things." On "things"? What kind of things? "Thinglike things," everyday things? Or is the emphasis on "experience"? *Which* are the simpler, more direct experiences? What *kinds* of experience are the inherently simpler kinds? By what standard is degree of simplicity or directness determined? Are the simpler experiences the more familiar ones? But highly involved experiences may be actually more familiar than "simpler" ones. (For example, an ongoing foreign war may be more familiar than the color magenta.) Are there atomic simples of experience which *compose* the experiential complexes? If so, no compelling view on the kind of being they are has ever been achieved. What with indefinables, indescribables, and ineffables widespread and vigorously entertained, we should no doubt have to say that the atoms must be present but are just not easily detectable in their purity.

The type of outlook according to which prose is "nearer to reflection" is also to be found in Santayana, for whom "prose has a great defect, which is abstractness." [7] Waiving the question whether this "defect" is unique to prose, we must ask by what standard is abstractness a defect. The standard of concreteness? Should we always aim not to speak abstractly? Should we aim to alter mathematics, philosophy, and all theoretical work in order to correct the defect? In Santayana's outlook there could be no point in saying that abstractness inhibits the poetic search for truth, for as we have seen, he believes that poetry "feigns" and embodies "false notions." From what at first appears to be a more detached standpoint, Whitehead says that "an abstraction is nothing else than an omission of part of the truth."[8] But can there be any kind of attempt to embody truth which, as finite and human, is not "an omission of part of the truth"?

In the two elaborated versions of concreteness here considered, the concrete is associated with the particular, the individual, the living, the organic, the immediate. How these notions are related to one another must depend to some extent upon implicit conventions. That they do not all require one another, and that they are not even necessarily compatible, is scarcely difficult to show. We have seen that the notion of the individual as "what is directly confronted in experience" is at the least misleading. Whatever else an individual is, it is a varied, uniquely ordered array of traits, and as an individual it might almost be said to be accessible in any way but "direct confrontation." If something like direct confrontation is what is intended by "immediate experience," then immediate experience is not of individuals. Is it experience of mere "particulars"? Assuming that a particular differs from other particulars in its sheer numerical distinctness, what reason is there to suppose that this distinctness is encountered in an unmediated way? The notion of unmediated "experience" implies that (1) *anything or nothing* is "confronted"; for to specify something implies comparison and therefore mediation. But looked at in another and contrasting way, if immediacy and direct confrontation of particulars are the same, we must accept (2) a very *limited* range of data—particular shades of red, particular flowers, particular sounds (already a group of quite unsimple traits). And then we get into trouble. For immediacy suggests the easily graspable. But particularity suggests the graspably distinct. So that to identify them as one and the same direct confrontation suggests (3) *both* a very limited range of data and an unlimited range of data. There are not only particular shades of red and the like; there are particular electrons, particular politicians, particular stars, particular explosions . . . particulars *ad infinitum*.

Immediate experience does not imply that what is experienced is living or organic. Nor does experience of the living and organic imply immediacy. Particularity or singleness does not imply individuality. Individuality does not imply life or organism. Individuality has no necessary connection with immediate experience.

ii

According to Hegel, poetry aims to bring together universality and individuality in its treatment of a "content." To be concerned with universality as such, disregarding that in which it is exemplified, is to engage in "abstract thought." To be concerned with individuality as such, disregarding its universal aspects, is to bypass "ideality" and remain within the unimaginative sphere of everyday consciousness. To link the two, to mediate between them, to reveal each as involving the other, is to achieve concreteness. Poetic imagination, Hegel says, "brings before our vision concrete reality rather than the abstract generalization."

These considerations provide only a formal use of the term "concrete." They tell us nothing about the method by which a content is treated concretely, or about what constitutes language that is concrete. Nor does the Hegelian text consistently adhere to this prescribed usage, in which concreteness results from a mediation of the universal and the individual. We find it saying, for instance, that "the imagination of the poet . . . must maintain a middle course between the abstract universality of pure thinking and the concrete corporeality of material objects." Here concreteness is identified not with a blending of extremes but with one of the extremes, an extreme formulated, moreover, in exceptionally limited terms. It may be that this usage is explainable as a failure of Hegel's student-editors, upon whose notes his posthumously published lectures on aesthetics (like other of his posthumous works) are partly based. But it may also be thought of perhaps as aberrant, in the qualified sense that

Hegel, eager to stress the inappropriateness of abstract thought dominating a poetic work, inadvertently leans to the other extreme and pulls the notion of concreteness with him. Aberrant or not, the usage raises (anew) the suspicion that at least in its application to poetry the idea of concreteness is much less clear in Hegel than his heavy reliance upon it would suggest.

We are told that the poetic work must provide us with "a concrete whole of idea, ends, actions, and events" or "a free and concrete coherence of all parts." The concreteness has much to do with the "unity" or "wholeness" achieved, and by and large it is equated with the kind of unity Hegel, like so many others, calls "organic." In a detailed attempt to illustrate the idea of concreteness, Hegel says:

[Poetry] helps us to approach the essential notion in its positive existence, the generic as clothed in its specific individuality. In the view of ordinary common sense I understand by language, both in its impression on my hearing or sight, the meaning in its immediacy, in other words, without receiving its image before the mind. The phrases, for instance "the sun," or "in the morning," possess each of them no doubt a distinct sense; but neither the Dawn [n]or the Sun are themselves made present to our vision. When, however, the poet says: "When now the dawning Eos soared heavenwards with rosy fingers," here without question we have the concrete fact brought home to us. The poetical expression adds, however, yet more, for it associates with the object recognized a vision of the same, or we should rather say the purely abstract relation of knowledge vanishes, and the real definition takes its place. In the same way take the phrase, "Alexander conquered the Persian empire." Here, no doubt, so far as content is concerned, we have a concrete conception; the many-sided definition of it, however, expressed here in the word "victory," is concentrated in a featureless and pure abstraction, which fails to image before us anything of the appearance and reality of the exploit accomplished by Alexander. This truth applies to every kind of similar expression. We recognize the bare fact; but it remains pale and dun, and from the point of view of individual existence undetermined and abstract. The poetic conception consequently embraces the fulness of the objective phenomenon as it essentially exists, and is able to elaborate the same united with the essential ideality of the fact in a creative totality.[9]

Does this explanation suffice to define the traits of language by which concreteness can be identified? In everyday discourse we protest that an account of a subject is abstract when it fails to provide an example that is accessible, or when it does not help us to be confronted with a spatio-temporal particular, or when nothing is denoted which could be considered actual. These protestations, however intended, are not all one and the same. To be given the example of a unicorn would provide accessibility of one kind but not of another. The unicorn might be regarded as a particular but would not usually be regarded as spatio-temporal; nor would it usually be regarded as actual. Everyday demands for concreteness are neither precise nor interesting, because in their expectations they are addicted to examples of actualities which are well-beaten, uncritical, and unrepresentative of the kinds that there *can* be. In terms of such demands, Homer's dawning Eos soaring heavenwards with rosy fingers would fail the concreteness test. The Hegelian conception seems to stress not only detail (though surely that) but vividness, figure, intensity, and perhaps novelty as aspects of concreteness. "Specificity," whether in Hegel or in popular expectation, is not very clear as a demand. What mode of the subject's being should be specified? Strictly, to specify is to name a species, that is, merely a universal of more limited scope.

For Hegel, the rosy-fingered goddess is a poetic paradigm. And his account as a whole remains paradigmatic rather than definitional in a more comprehensive sense. He requires images as prerequisites of concreteness. But there are different types of images, and whether every type would subserve concreteness in his or in any sense, is a fair question. Aside from the type of images, should it be said that a minimal number of images is required in a poetic work for the achievement of concreteness? Does concreteness admit of degree, and if so, is there a specifiable minimum degree?

Two points must be pushed. (1) Hegel's aesthetics of poetry sees linguistic expressions, expressions belonging to the language used, as poor or rich, pale or vivid, in themselves and before they are dealt with by the poet. And (2) his contention that poetry as such must be concrete becomes doctrinaire and empty in the face of much actual poetry

(1) To Hegel "morning" is an indifferent word, plain, colorless, and unexciting. But surely as a mere word it is neither more nor less concrete than "rosy fingers." Beyond its universally accepted connotation, its role is determined by the poet, or by the poetic work sometimes in spite of the poet; it is made subordinate or made dominant. It has no intrinsic status in a scale of concreteness, nor has any other term. Its typical function in everyday speech may be preserved or transformed, diminished or augmented, poetically.

> Full many a glorious morning have I seen
> Flatter the mountain tops with sovereign eye,
> Kissing with golden face the meadows green,
> Gilding pale streams with heavenly alchemy.[10]

In Hegelian terms it would be appropriate to say that "morning" here is concretized, as it were, by the "determinations" of the succeeding lines. There is nothing inherently objectionable in this way of approaching the matter. But "morning" can be seen in a different and quite opposite role, namely, as the source or agent, rather than as the recipient, of determination. Its location in the poem is such as to open up the world. In an everyday context, and in everyday sense, the sun at *any* time of day can light up the mountains and the meadows. But Shakespeare's sun is the morning sun, and "morning" is as determinative as its (poetic) effects and concomitants are; to it belongs the sovereign eye. Can "morning" be regarded as an "image"? As "present to our vision"? It doesn't seem to matter. An image, like a word, is not "there" to be incorporated for what it is worth; its function and value is achieved in the poetic work, and there may be no exact cluster of words which determines it. By virtue of its prior locations in perspectives which remain dimly associated with it, the mere idea of morning, unlocated in any specific perspective, can provoke the spontaneous feeling either of brightness and newness or of timidity and primitiveness. But it can be made to bind everything else together by the discovered intricacy of its being. In just this way does it dominate the consciousness of King Henry VI, pausing and ruminating in his solitary flight from hatred.

> This battle fares like to the morning's war,
> When dying clouds contend with growing light,
> What time the shepherd, blowing of his nails,
> Can neither call it perfect day nor night.
> Now sways it this way, like a mighty sea
> Forced by the tide to combat with the wind;
> Now sways it that way, like the selfsame sea
> Forced to retire by fury of the wind:
> Sometime the flood prevails, and then the wind;
> Now one the better, then another best;
> Both tugging to be victors, breast to breast;
> Yet neither conqueror nor conquered:
> So is the equal poise of this fell war.[11]

Contingency, indecisiveness, instability, all in the womb of morning, define a person and his life, and the world that he endures.

(2) Poetry does not require "positive existence" or "specific individuality." It does not require "concrete fact," definite images, predominantly "sensory" images, or "real" definitions.

> Let the bird of loudest lay,
> On the sole Arabian tree,
> Herald sad and trumpet be,
> To whose sound chaste wings obey.

A congregation of birds has been summoned, to mourn the mysterious death and contemplate the mysterious life of two of their kind. In the immediate sequel, time, individual existence, and space, are recognized only through reference to certain birds of familiar character.

> From this session interdict
> Every fowl of tyrant wing,
> Save the eagle, feather'd king;
> Keep the obsequy so strict.
>
> Let the priest in surplice white,
> That defunctive music can,
> Be the death-divining swan,
> Lest the requiem lack his right.

The conspicuous traits of the eagle and the swan accentuate by contrast the transcendent traits of the Phoenix and the Dove. From this point on, the visible world and Hegel's principles are left behind.

> Here the anthem doth commence:
> Love and constancy is dead;
> Phoenix and the Turtle fled
> In a mutual flame from hence.
>
> So they lov'd, as love in twain
> Had the essence but in one;
> Two distincts, division none;
> Number there in love was slain.
>
> Hearts remote, yet not asunder;
> Distance and no space was seen
> 'Twixt this Turtle and his queen:
> But in them it were a wonder.
>
> So between them love did shine,
> That the Turtle saw his right
> Flaming in the Phoenix' sight;
> Either was the other's mine.
>
> Property was thus appalled
> That the self was not the same;
> Single nature's double name
> Neither two nor one was called.

> Reason, in itself confounded,
> Saw division grow together,
> To themselves yet either neither,
> Simple were so well compounded:
>
> That it cried, How true a twain
> Seemeth this concordant one!
> Love hath reason, reason none,
> If what parts, can so remain.[12]

Do we find here the "vision" of a "concrete fact"? There are no images of individuals, and no sensory images of relations. The understandable recourse is to think of the poetry as "abstract" in the extreme. But poetry of this kind cannot be stereotyped. And there is no explanatory or analytical advantage in calling the poem an abstract whole, any more than there is in calling it a concrete whole. The linguistic tissue and the level of discrimination do not lend themselves to these categories. Must the polarity of abstractness-concreteness be relevant to poetry? Or might it be precisely the irrelevance of the very distinction involved that, once perceived, helps to clarify the poetic process?

Hegel, requiring the concrete artistic product to be an "organic whole," requires the content selected for it to have "intrinsic unity." What constitutes such unity, the unity of a content "in itself" (*in sich selbst*)? There are many kinds of unity and many respects in which unity can be said to obtain. Whatever is called unitary in some respect may also not be unitary in some other respect. Is "intrinsic" unity that which is one in every possible respect? Plainly, we need an illustration, though we can confidently predict that none will be forthcoming. Aristotle, for whom the model of a living organism already provides the ideal of poetic unity, is aware of different kinds of unity, but cannot help thinking of them as if they were degrees of unity, so that some are deemed by him to have a truer unity than others. Thus epic poetry has "less unity" than tragic poetry. Thus also the circle, of all lines, is the most "truly one."[13]

If a poetic content is to be regarded as a unity, is it preserved *as* a unity when it is embodied in the poetic process? Does it remain a unity in the same *respect* in which it was a unity when imported into the process? *Can* it remain a unity in the same respect? To ask, once again, how we are to ascertain the property in question, in this case the unitariness or the kind of unitariness, is to raise only one problem. Another problem is why we must agitate ourselves about whether the content is a unity.

The conception of a content not as adopted whole and eligible for use but as shaped or even engendered within the process of poetic invention, facilitates the resolution of the question about unity. Whatever kind of unity is attributed to a subject *for* poetry will not necessarily be attributable to the subject as embodied. If the traits of the subject embodied need not conform to the traits of the subject envisaged, neither need the type of unity, which is one possible trait. The approach of Hegel and countless others who are attracted by the concept of unity is legislative. That is, they are not primarily concerned to ask themselves whether poetry as written or spoken, as practised, needs the concept of unity in order to be justly and adequately understood as poetry. They are more concerned with establishing a norm and saying what must be the case. The concept of the unitary, like that of the real, is one of the grand eulogistic concepts. It would not do for plurality and diversity to be as fundamental or more fundamental than unity in the constitution of subjects. That would be to imply "disunity," which carries the very sound of evil.

IV

ON VARIOUS
CONTRASTS OF
POETRY AND PROSE

i

Probably no one has ever been entirely comfortable with the traditional distinction between poetry and prose, since no one wishes dogmatically to identify poetry with verse, and prose can be a configurative guise which poetry assumes. T. S. Eliot says: "I have never come across a final, comprehensive, and satisfactory account of the difference between poetry and prose. We can distinguish between prose and verse, and between verse and poetry; but the moment the intermediate term *verse* is suppressed, I do not believe that any distinction between prose and poetry is meaningful." [1] It has long been contended that verse, besides not being a necessary condition for poetry, is not a sufficient condition. Aristotle holds that Homer and Empedocles had nothing in common except the meter they used. The Bible is the clearest evidence that a distinction between the poetic and the prosaic cannot be correlated with formal properties of word-arrangement. In the light of such considerations, some have suggested that the meaningful contrast, so far as poetry is concerned, is between poetry and science (e.g., Wordsworth, Coleridge), or between poetry and logic (e.g., Shelley). Yet these latter types of contrast pay no attention to essential differences *within* literary art.

Somehow the need to contrast poetry and prose, using these very terms, has survived, and in fact has never lapsed. Coleridge and Shelley, despite their reservations, continued to speak of poetry and prose. The explanation is not difficult. The effective contrast, that which emerges if not that which is actually held in view, is between a poetic and a non-poetic use of language, regardless of whether the latter subserves scientific or artistic purposes and regardless of whether it is the language of a biological hypothesis or of a novel. The term "prose" continues to be used because it is most economically suited for the purpose. It has come to *mean* "non-poetic language," and contrasts that are made dwell upon properties of poetic and properties of non-poetic language. The more customary contrast too had been one of properties; but it had confused forms of linguistic utterance with the physical appearance of these forms, and it had left no room for a distinction between poetry and poems. The various oppositions we have previously considered, those set up between the language appropriate for feelings and the language appropriate for events; the language of concreteness and the language of abstract thought; the language of quality and the language of practicality; the language of the organic and the language of the analytic—are thus all versions of the distinction between poetry and "prose."

To represent the working sense of the distinction as most clearly a contrast of poetic and non-poetic language, does not at all imply that poetry is nothing but "poetic language." It does not imply that *either* poetry or prose is to be understood in terms of language alone. But neither does it tolerate the view that poetry need not have to do with words, and that there is a "poetic sentiment" (Poe) which may be manifested, for instance, in music as well as in words; which in fact is better manifested in music than in words. The problem, as we shall see, is rather to show what it is in poetry, besides its words, that explains both why there has to be the kind of language there is and why the language takes on the character that it does.

ii

Poetry, it has been said, essentially differs from prose in being its own justification, an end in itself. Prose is a means to an end other than itself. Thus Hegel believes that, as distinguished from

the judgments and conclusions of the understanding, where we find that whether regarded theoretically as science or with reference to practical conduct and action, the main stress is on the final result,

poetry places equal if not greater value "on the path by which [the result] is reached." A similar contrast is made by Paul Valéry. Prose, he thinks, aims at establishing a "meaning" or a conclusion. Once that is established, it is annulled or swallowed up. The language it has used no longer matters, and therefore in a sense never did matter as language. The "form" of prose language is indifferent, replaceable, instrumental. Having accomplished its communicative function, prose is "translated . . . into nonlanguage." Poetry, on the other hand, whether or not it has a "use" beyond itself as language, must be preserved in precisely the same words and the same form; in these words and in this form lie its value.

In the practical or abstract uses of language that is specifically *prose*, the form is not preserved, does not outlive understanding, but dissolves in the light, for it has acted, it has made itself understood, it has lived. . . . But the poem, on the contrary, does not die for having been of use; it is purposely made to be reborn from its ashes and perpetually to become what it has been. . . . it tends to reproduce itself in its own form, it stimulates our minds to reconstruct it as it is.[2]

Valéry believes that he strengthens his distinction by comparing prose to walking and poetry to dancing. One would like to think that the analogy of dancing is an implicit attempt to interpret the old concept of "measure" in poetry as comprising more than "patterned language," language with an aspect of "repeat."[3] The dance is movement not limited to regular local progression; it is, presumably, the kind of measure, the kind of pattern, that cannot be found in prose. But so far as the suggestiveness of the analogy is concerned, there are many kinds of walking, and there are many kinds of dancing. It would seem as plausible to think of poetry in terms of stately walking as to think of poetry in terms of belly-dancing.

Unmentioned in the terms of Valéry's distinction between poetry and prose is the non-poetic language of various forms of literary art. Valéry's opinion notwithstanding, such language is prized for what it is and for its own sake, with the form that it has. It means what it means throughout its span of expression and communication. Its meaning is not something beyond it, something at which it aims, as one might aim to deliver a message to one's neighbor no matter how, but coincides with the unfolding of the language that constitutes the work as a whole. A novel reaches neither more nor less of a conclusion than a poem does, whether in the sense of a completion or in the sense of a substantive outcome.

The position before us speaks of "the practical or abstract uses of language" as if it did not matter whether these uses were basically the same or not. There is reason to believe that in Valéry (as in Eastman) the practical and the utilitarian are not regarded as appreciably different from the abstract, so far as a contrast with poetry is concerned. For the chief non-poetic role is assigned by him to the familiar, everyday functions of language. The scientific is treated as if it were the technological. No attention whatever is given to the language of philosophy, the language of its forms, levels, or styles. Even what is taken to be utilitarian or practical language is construed along the narrowest of lines, as if it were all reducible to the pattern of conveying a danger signal. There is a tacit supposition that the paradigm of "prose" is to be found in oral speech, which naturally "dissolves" when its point is made. This stacks the cards in favor of the integrity of poetic language, for poetry is not thought of as being on the same plane of oral spontaneity and improvisation. We must ask: Is the prose of a psychological case history practical and utilitarian? Is it necessarily abstract? What about a work of history in the usual sense, for instance a political history of Spain in the sixteenth century? Utilitarian? Abstract? And what about a work of jurisprudence, or the prose of a statute, or a contract? Can these be classified in Valéry's simple world of prose?

To think that we can separate a meaning or a conclusion from the body of a prose work, from the language which achieves that meaning and conclusion, is to think of language as if it were assemblable like a pipe with many sections put together, and through which gas is pumped to a destination. Except for repeated use, the pipe is valueless and disposable. It does not affect and is not affected by what is piped. Maybe the appropriate analogy is to think of a meaning in prose as if it were a hot potato passed out at a picnic and juggled impatiently and hastily till it reaches the right person. Or—to assume fitting sobriety—should we think of it as if it were a discreetly handled verdict, one already known but requiring to be transported in the wraps of conventional rhetoric?

Does what we are expected to concede consist in the familiar thought that it is possible for prose to convey one and the "same" meaning through different word-combinations? Before compromising our doubts, let us suggest (*a*) that we assume this to be true only where we are inclined to *stress* sameness rather than difference and are willing to overlook differences as negligible; (*b*) that a circumstance wherein different prose versions serve as possible means to the "same" end is not *typical* of prose but obtains primarily where meanings are familiar and gross rather than subtle, far-reaching, or precise; and (*c*) that we can find a parallel in poetry; for it is often the experience of poets themselves that substantially the "same" poetic objective can be attained, if not always with equal satisfaction (any more than in prose), by varying their words in continuing experimental efforts.

A verbal form or order, and any of the various kinds of se-
quential force, in the language of law, physical theory, philos-
ophy, or history, is coextensive with a meaning as it develops. As
much or as little of this prose language "dies" in the process of
communication as does the language of poetry. Verbal and ordi-
nal variations within it are conceivable. But they are conceivable
in poetry. The morality of linguistic alteration ordinarily dictates
that anything is permissible before Publication: changing around
the paragraphs of a philosophic work, or re-arranging the stanzas
of a poem. When the product acquires Public status in a physically
fixed form, it is treated indelicately but charitably if it is prose,
its parts being freely selected and independently assessed. If it is
poetry, especially if it is short, it is treated as an "organic whole,"
and its imperfections are likely to be regarded as fatal. In a view
like Valéry's, a poem and only a poem is integral and sacrosanct.
Valéry himself might have been pained to know that men some-
times have had quite other and much firmer images of literary
integrity—of the integrity of systematic works in philosophy,
and of an inevitable structure in these works. To them, the order
of the Parts in Spinoza's *Ethics* or the order of the Questions and
Articles in St. Thomas Aquinas compares to the form of a poetic
work as a magisterial procession compares to dancing. There are
many who would wish to put the matter in another light, by
asking: if we take random specimens of poetry on the one hand,
and of a closely reasoned piece of theoretical inquiry on the
other, is there not a sense in which the sequential order of the
words and sounds in the poems might have to be called gratui-
tous while that of the theoretical works might have to be called
necessary or compelling? Such a question has its own serious
problems: it tends to think of the sequence of poetic words as
being less firm than the logical sequence, instead of being dif-
ferently firm. But it reveals in its own way the weakness of
Valéry's approach.

It has often been held that the sensuous texture of poetry,
including its dimension of sound, is what makes its language

incomparable and uniquely inviolable. But an equally plausible conviction would be understandable for scientific prose or for metaphysics, stated this way: the concatenation of relevant ideas, the chain of reasoning, the extended perception, the specific formulation, of a scientific or metaphysical work is marked by a structuring of language that is incomparable and inviolable. If there are doubts about such a conception of scientific or philosophic prose, they only match corresponding doubts about the language of poetry. If it is not true that all science and philosophy expresses itself linguistically to the effect described, neither does all poetry or all poetic language rest upon sensuous texture.

These difficulties help to show why it is also precarious to say that in prose the emphasis is upon *what* is meant in words, and that in poetry the emphasis is upon *how* the words mean. These two dimensions are mutually relevant. We cannot think in an adequate way of science, philosophy, and history mainly in terms of what they are dealing with and only minimally in terms of how they are dealing with it. And we cannot tenably say that how poetry uses words subordinates the importance of what is being grasped or constructed by these words.

A widespread version of the Valéry-type of contrast is that a prose work can be "translated" and a poem "really" cannot. (1) If by "translated" is meant "rendered in another social language," the contention is simply false. Works of prose and poetry alike have been translated, sometimes with universal approbation and sometimes less happily, sometimes with a sense of adequacy and sometimes with a sense of newly acquired value or independent gain. There always will be those who declare that poetry "just cannot" be translated. But there always will be historical and philosophical critics also who declare the same to be true of works in philosophy—that the language of Aristotle, for example, cannot be adequately translated from the Greek. (2) If by "translated" is meant "rendered in other words within the *same* social language," the foregoing reflections on Valéry, which suggest the parallels between poetry and prose, are applicable. (3) And if, finally, "translation" is used—as we shall use it—in a broader and more comprehensive sense, as that aspect of articulation in which a work is made accessible and made continuingly relatable, then all criticism is a mode of translation, and not poetry alone but all human products whatever are translatable.

iii

Coleridge, doubting that a significant distinction between poetry and prose can be based primarily upon the study of words and word-patterns, looks to other factors. What sustains the poetic character of a work, what defines its movement, is "the property of exciting a more continuous and equal attention than the language of prose aims at, whether colloquial or written." [4] This property is elsewhere described by him as "the use of language natural to us in a state of excitement." [5] One side of Coleridge had felt that poetry could be regarded as dedicating itself to "the communication of immediate pleasure," in contrast to science, which is dedicated to the acquisition and communication of truth. Another side of him felt that this account was unsound, for not only poetry but literary prose would be thus distinguished from science. It never did occur to him that, even beyond literary prose, various other kinds of non-poetic language might communicate and even aim to communicate immediate pleasure. Nor did it occur to him that the concept of pleasure, mediate or immediate, might not be adequate to encompass the types of satisfaction or the magnitude of the response aroused by superior poetry. Actually, the formulation which additionally stresses "language natural to us in a state of excitement" is even less adequate. It is hard to limit the notion of excitement in the way needed. Language of many kinds, including strikingly non-poetic language, can be natural to us (an "us" that is culturally and emotionally variable) in a state of excitement.

Yet the general idea of poetry "exciting a more continuous and equal attention than the language of prose aims at," though as vulnerable as the other formulations and as devoid of helpful qualification, contains hidden depths. In a sense it embraces the point that Valéry and others try to make, but being freer of false optimism, it is able to suggest this point more flexibly. Perhaps the Coleridgean idea can be formulated in the following way. A work of poetry does not engage our attention in an atmosphere of preconceptions, of expectations such as are likely to be attached to works in the language of prose. It is not committed to and not hampered by standard grammatical forms. Nor is it beholden to publicly approved canons of clarity and effectiveness in language. We do not say, of a poem, that it is written *in* "good verse," in the manner that we approve of a theoretical work as being written *in* "good prose." Prose cannot wholly divest itself of formal syntactical props, not to mention familiar phrases, that are expected to facilitate communication. The props, the standardized phrases, are taken for granted. They do not require attention from those whom they address, and although they are needed toward the linguistic achievement of meaning, they are not comparable with other word-combinations in the expression of what is important. Poetic language, on the other hand, excites "a more continuous and equal attention" because we both approach it and follow it with a tense strategy toward what is to come, what we may encounter at any moment, and the way in which it may be encountered. Though we do come prepared to identify the words of poetry by an initial (and standard) response of association, we are ready to modify these initial associations, and are ready to deal with other unusual verbal impulsions. Thus we credit every word in poetry with the possibility of an important role. Unheralded particles, for instance, may carry a heavy weight. And we are ready to accept a climate of mystery for the emergence of meaning or feeling. In prose we wish to be launched securely and to move forward, not indeed to an expected destination nor at any preassigned pace, but in a manner which ensures successiveness and makes us aware of it.

If this is the burden of Coleridge's differentiating principle, it must be respected more as an insight into the psychology and natural history of communication than as a mapping of boundaries in two types of discipline. We remain doubtful that the attitude attributed to prose would apply clearly in a work, say, like *Biographia Literaria;* that the attitude attributed to poetry would apply clearly in Homer or the epics of the Bible. Whether, in contrast to prose, poetry *can* divest itself of all formal props, may be a moot question. But the formulaic elements in Homer and the recurrent stylized phrases of the Old Testament demonstrate that poetry can use such props to powerful effect. Coleridge's general viewpoint fortunately does not require that prose be regarded as merely instrumental and poetry as self-enclosed and self-articulating. At the same time, it fails to explain why poetic language should foster the kind of tension that it does.

A rather different approach is attempted in Hegel's analysis of the relation between poetry and prose.[6] For Hegel as for Coleridge a contrast cannot be reached by scrutinizing words and phrases. Poetry and prose must be seen as "two distinct spheres of consciousness." Poetry is the consciousness of the infinite "life of Spirit," consciousness of the many forms of consciousness: passions, ideals, exploits, and aims. Prose is the consciousness of the world "external" to Spirit, the world of cause and effect, means and ends, facts in their relation to one another. It is the consciousness belonging to the "understanding," probing a world of "limited categories" and of the finite, represented as finite. Although poetry can deal with any subject whatever, including facts and events, present times and past, of the physical world, it deals with these subjects only as pertinent to an interest of mind, as an expression of spiritual energy, as an occasion of the power of thought and feeling. Neither prose nor poetry is

close to "ordinary consciousness." Both are, however, related to
it genetically and through the functions they perform. Thus, con-
tinues Hegel, prose may be said to widen, poetry to deepen as
well as widen, ordinary consciousness. Poetry, drawing on the
"imagination," is liberating to consciousness. Prose (natural
science, factual understanding) is qualifying and restricting. It
considers traits only in their dependence upon other traits, and
in their aspects of relativity. Poetry, concerned above all with
concrete and organic wholes, therefore depicts all of its objects
as independent, free, unitary, self-determined. The prosaic con-
sciousness seeks to discover the laws of phenomena, "the laws
themselves under this view tending to harden from each other
in their isolate singularity." Poetry makes man conscious of
"what he is and by what he is surrounded." Man "must recog-
nize the powers by which he is driven or influenced; and it is just
such a knowledge which poetry, in its original and vital form,
supplies."

In a perspective like this, imagination is once more the domain
from which non-poetic disciplines are excluded. And then it be-
comes virtually impossible to interpret what takes place when
new ideas, new insights, new possible models for explanation
and schematization, enter into scientific awareness. The view
of laws of physical existence as remaining separate and com-
partmentalized flies in the face of overwhelming evidence to the
contrary, the history of natural science revealing a trend toward
the interrelation of laws, toward the systematizing and unifying
of results stemming from special inquiries. That theoretical
knowledge of any kind, scientific or other, should be thought of
as enclosing consciousness and curtailing its sense of freedom
betrays a serious confusion. To become conscious of more and
more dependencies, conditional traits, and limiting relations
within the physical world—for that matter, within the world
at large—implies not that we are reduced or subjected to these
conditions, but rather that we increase the kind of intellectual
control called explanation. And this kind is basic not merely for

technological control but for the possibility of increased self-control.

Hegel thinks of explanatory understanding as merely juxta-posing particular existence and general law, but of poetry as achieving the sense of genuine wholeness. Poetry he sees as radiating the warmth of Spirit; understanding, as chilling con-sciousness by an introduction of the "external." But why must the relation between poetic and non-poetic consciousness be thus depicted as one of mutual repugnance? Why should man's know-ledge of himself and his surroundings be thought to be supplied exclusively or even primarily by poetry? Are we speaking of what we have found to be knowledge in the minimal sense of that which proves applicable and extensible, or are we speaking of what we think should be regarded as knowledge? Affective reaction to scientific inquiry varies from age to age and even from generation to generation, but who can seriously demon-strate the irrelevance of factual understanding to the question of "the powers by which man is driven or influenced"? For poetry to be given so fundamental a role in human self-illumination is, to be sure, an impressive measure of the distance between Hegel and those before or after him who have worried themselves about poetry's "lies." The healthful distance would not be abbre-viated by a recognition that knowledge yielded poetically and knowledge yielded prosaically may co-exist for human gain. Al-though the two spheres of consciousness are incommensurable in a methodological sense—there is no standard by which a con-tribution in one sphere is made relevant to actual productive procedure in the other—they are complementary in a human sense. It is better for men to be able to live in both spheres than in only one; it is better for them that the world is accessible in (at least) two aspects each illimitably variegated. From the van-tage point of either sphere, it has of course been common human practice to revile the other for its supposed deceptiveness. Verily, man is the animal with the freedom to contemn its own resources.

Another attempt to ground a contrast of poetry and prose in

the larger setting of the human process is made by Dewey, for whom forms of "consciousness" give way to forces of "experience."

While there is no difference that may be exactly defined between prose and poetry, there is a gulf between the prosaic and poetic as extreme limiting terms of tendencies in experience. One of them realizes the power of words to express what is in heaven and earth and under the seas by means of extension; the other by intension. The prosaic is an affair of description and narration, of details accumulated and relations elaborated. It spreads as it goes like a legal document or catalogue. The poetic reverses the process. It condenses and abbreviates, thus giving words an energy of expansion that is almost explosive. A poem presents material so that it becomes a universe in itself, one, which, even when it is a miniature whole, is not embryonic any more than it is labored through argumentation. There is something self-enclosed and self-limiting in a poem. . . .[7]

The use of the terms "intension" and "extension" poses difficulties. Does not the view that poetry expresses what it expresses by intension leave open the implication that it refers to nothing or applies to nothing? Is the careless implication to be allowed that there is any kind of prose which is wholly designative or referential? To speak of the prosaic as "an affair of description and narration" overlooks the existence of the vast amount of poetry which is not only descriptive and narrative in *some* sense, but which is often detailed to an extent unusual in prose. To say that prose spreads like a catalogue is false to the prose of many philosophers, novelists, and scientists. Prose and poetry alike "spread" in the sense that they unfold spatially and temporally in the process of communication. The idea that poetry "condenses and abbreviates," if it is an acceptable idea in some respect, cannot imply a "reversal" of the process whereby detail is multiplied. "Condensing and abbreviating," whatever else it may imply, can refer only to the *way* in which details are *wrought*, not to the reduction of their number. Reducing the number of details *can* be a literary stratagem—but of either poetry or prose.

In observing that poetic language, like non-poetic, can take the form of "describing," we must back away from the precipice that recurrently threatens us. The way is left open for the question, are the descriptions true or not? And the way is then left open for the question, do works of poetry make truth-claims? If they do not affirm propositions explicitly, do they affirm them implicitly? W. M. Urban, among others, contends that propositional commitment is inevitable in poetry.[8] He insists that Shelley's lines "Life, like a dome of many coloured glass,/ Stains the white radiance of Eternity,/ Until death tramples it to fragments," affirm one proposition and deny another; for might the lines not have said that life does *not* stain the white radiance of Eternity? Well, what if Shelley's lines somehow had been arranged to include the "not"? Would we have debated about its truth, about which of two alternatives was the true one? Or would we instead have sought to grasp *that* angle of discrimination? Sir Philip Sidney's principle that the poet "nothing affirms" does not say that the poet nothing perceives. The principle means to suggest the irrelevance to poetry of truth-claims and confirmation-processes, of what Urban prefers to call the process of "authentication." This term reflects Urban's attempt to recognize a value-affirmation that he tells us the poem necessarily includes in its implicit propositions. Since, however, poets are not required to prove anything, or to cite evidence in behalf of their words, some philosophers have sought to re-define truth in art (and poetry in particular) as non-propositional, thereby hoping to avoid the embarrassment of artistic testing and at the same time to preserve the idea of "authenticity." Authenticity suggests the kind of justification which imposes adherence to established norms. It suggests a lingering struggle to make poetry rival science without emulating it. The apologetic tradition is thus seen in its militant phase, in quest of a counterpart to the evidential compulsion by which science can smile upon mere good taste and radiate iron authority.

V

POETIC JUDGMENT
AND POETIC
QUERY

i

We are now prepared to build a structure that will house the assumptions and reasons by which the preceding analysis has been guided. Some of the raw materials have been forged in the course of criticism. Loose ground and dubious ways have been identified. But patience is necessary if we wish to construct soundly. The unique aspects of poetry and its language cannot be ascertained without exploring the roots which it shares with other basic forms of human production, roots which lie deep in the human process. The history of poetic theory shows by its own example that little can be built without, first of all, an adequate substructure; and this is what we must now try to provide. Before being able to say what the poet accomplishes as poet, it is necessary to reflect on what the poet and his undertaking are as human complexes and as complexes of art.

Man is the possibility exemplified by men—the natural complex of possibility continuingly actualized and yet reciprocally modified by its actualizations. And men are creatures—that is, they arise in the world and are related to the world, and there are specific conditions without which they cannot arise. The natural complex which we vaguely call the world is constituted by innumerable traits or sub-complexes, including relations. These complexes intersect and overlap, also in innumerable ways. Each, merely as such, comprises an order with its own integrity. Each is an order of traits, an order of sub-complexes. There is no reason to believe in sub-complexes which are finally non-complex and thus without sub-complexes of their own. For there is no reason to believe that relations somewhere come to an end. We have to note well a certain implication of this approach, namely, that each complex, as an order of traits, in *some* respect constitutes an order of intelligibility. However small or large the scope of this order or province may be, it forms a sphere of relevance which obtains among the traits that constitute it. Each man is an order of complexes, and so (on another level) is man; and each, therefore, comprises innumerable sub-orders. Every one of them has a definable character, an integrity. There is an order that consists in the individual man as a whole, but there is also a sub-order that consists in his nervous system. Ordinarily, the nervous system is made intelligible in terms of the larger order to which it belongs. But to *some* extent and in *some* respect, the nervous system is itself a sphere of intelligibility; to that extent, it is *not* solely a constituent of the larger order. Its inclusion in the larger order is one of the traits that form its own integrity—a trait that it has in *common* with other complexes. Its inclusion of sub-orders of its own is also one of the traits that form its integrity—a trait that *distinguishes* it from other complexes.

There is an order of waking and an order of sleeping, and in each an order of dreaming; an order of hearing and an order of touching, a gastro-intestinal order and an economic order, a terrestrial order and a celestial order, an ecclesiastical order and a deer-hunting order. . . . And these, again, can intersect or overlap (though often not in any picturable way)—that is, they can have points or areas (traits and conditions) in common. A complex has as many kinds of traits as there are orders in which it functions (in which it is "located," to which it "belongs"). A man who is a banker, father, tennis-player, and Republican is located in four orders (among innumerable others in which he is located). Each location helps to constitute him as the individual he is; it helps to constitute his integrity as an individual. But he also has an integrity in each location. The orders of human existence and functioning, as distinguished from orders which include no human traits, no human forms of existence, are perspectival orders or perspectives. A man who is a banker and a father is located in or occupies the perspective of banking and the perspective of fatherhood.

The most inclusive perspective of the human individual is what is commonly called his life. "A life," without further definition, suggests sometimes a biological totality, sometimes the temporal span of an organism between birth and death. Although it is a conception that we cannot dispense with, by itself it does not suggest what is peculiarly and comprehensively human. The tendency then is to think of conscious life, and especially that aspect of it called self-conscious life, as the essential perspective or human order. Some who have made "experience" the category distinctively applicable to man have thought of it as the process or the course of conscious life; plurally, within this approach, "experiences" become moments or incidents within conscious life. Now in whatever way we may wish to deal with the notion of experience, or whether we wish to use it at all, there are complexes of a human individual that are not complexes of consciousness and yet are fundamental to him as an individual and as human; for example, many of his relations to other individuals, and many of the possibilities that are his whether he is aware of them or not. (It is equally true that there are complexes of a human *community* that are not complexes of consciousness and yet are fundamental to it as a community. But we may restrict ourselves here to the individual, with the assumption that the individual perspective and the communal perspective, though distinguishable, are inseparable and equally basic.) The human complexes which are not complexes of consciousness take the form of patterns and relations which help to constitute a being as human. They are not components of consciousness. They need not enter "into" consciousness. Yet to describe them as "living processes" would not be to describe them satisfactorily in all their aspects. It is the need to do justice to these relations and patterns that prompts care in identifying the most comprehensive perspective—the most inclusive order of an individual's being.

This perspective is not "in" a man, and certainly not in his "mind." We speak here rather of a man as being "in" a perspective; but in *this* perspective he always is. The being of a man is not conceivable apart from the order of his being. But the being or order is ill-interpreted when regarded primarily as a totality (of traits). It is directional. It embraces processes and relations, actual and possible. The boundaries of the order are never fully determinate. When any of its possibilities is actualized, other and different possibilities obtain in the new actualities, and so on without cessation of variety. A human order is subject to both modification and fortification by the world within which it is one among many. Considered in so far as it is, by an irregular progression, fortified or modified, this order is (a man's) experience. Considered in so far as it is bounded by time, space, and society, this order is a (man's) history.

The order that constitutes a human being (or human being) is itself located in wider, more pervasive orders. For a man or any other natural complex to be located in or included in such an order is to share traits that are of wider scope. Any order, any complex includes and is included in other orders. There is no privileged order of being, no inherently primary order. Another way of saying this is: any order may be primary in a given respect. Thus the order of a man's consciousness is one among the countless orders of the world, and one among the orders that go to make up his being. It may become primary, however, when men stand in a relation to other complexes which are felt, or of which they are aware. It is the kind of order, and presumably the only kind, which can define its own limits, and which can define

the form of primacy belonging to other orders. A man can con-
sciously conceive of the complexes constituting his consciousness
as being also located in other orders apart from his consciousness
and pre-dating his consciousness. Consider, further, the order of
feelings and occurrences that are private to a man. This is not an
order completely *sui generis*. It is a sub-order of other more com-
prehensive orders. Ontologically, it is a natural complex in the
same sense as the galactic or the economic order is, with its own
integrity. And this order of private complexes may contain, as
one of these private complexes, the intention of communicating
some of them; that is, introducing them into a non-private order.
As a private order, its primacy may consist in providing the
dominant conditions that motivate a scientist, a poet, a robber.

The most comprehensive perspective of a human being is the
order of all complexes which constitute him an integrity, which
make him that being, a being similar to many others, yet differ-
entiated from any other. These complexes collectively constitute
the order of *his* being. We could describe any given complex as
related or not related to him. A complex which is related to him
as a constituent of him in the sense just mentioned exemplifies
strong relevance. A complex is strongly relevant to an individual
when it is a determinant of either the preservation or the modi-
fication of his integrity; when it is relevant to him as an indi-
vidual, that individual. There are complexes related to an indi-
vidual not as *that* individual but as a complex undistinguished
from other individuals. This type of relatedness is *weak rele-
vance*. We may, then, define the most inclusive perspective of a
human individual as the order of all complexes strongly relevant
to that individual. The solar system, space, entropy, would (ordi-
narily) be complexes weakly relevant to an individual as such, in
so far as they are related to all individuals indifferently. A chance
encounter, a feeling of joy, a pain in the back, a love affair, a law-
suit, a theory of space that he has formulated, would (ordinarily)
be complexes strongly relevant to an individual, altering or en-
trenching his integrity. A complex weakly relevant to an indi-

vidual-as-an-*individual* (e.g., the solar system) may be strongly
relevant to that individual-as-an-*existence*. The integrity which
is affected or determined would then be that of an existing com-
plex (of whatever kind), not that of an individuated complex.

We are not talking about what is "inside" an individual's ex-
perience or "outside" of it, or about the "inner" and "outer"
world of an individual. We are talking about an individual. And
about the world that constitutes that individual—which is neces-
sarily a sub-complex or sub-order of the world at large. We are
talking about orders which overlap or are distinct from each
other. What is "in" any order is what is relevant to it.

ii

A man's being acquires its essential character from two sources:
the circumstances which befall him and the ways in which he
judges the world. And the essential character of the world in so
far as its relation to a man's being is concerned (in so far as it is
"his" world) it acquires through the ways in which he judges it.
These ways of judging inevitably derive from and are dependent
upon more pervasive conditions than a man's own being pro-
vides. But they are the ways in which man grasps, delineates,
bounds, and exposes his being and his world; they are the de-
fining processes, the continuing definitions, of his being and his
world.

The products of a man's life and history—described most ge-
nerically as his acts or deeds, his assertions or declarations, and
his contrivances—are his judgments. Such are the complexes
that constitute utterance. To the extent that a man can be said to
be the product of other natural complexes, he does not judge. To
the extent that any complexes can be said to be his product, he
judges. As in many fundamental distinctions, the borderline is
not easy to draw, and the specific determinations that depend
upon its being drawn are numerous. This much can be said se-
curely: certain conditions under which a man is product are

themselves owing to his having produced in a way that he did. And certain conditions under which a man produces are owing to his having been product in a way that he was. No human product owes its being entirely to its producer or producers: the world of a producer must allow the production, that is, provide the conditions for it. On the other hand, products arising under conditions in which a man is entirely unconscious may yet be his products, for they may be attributed to what he has become and is, to what *his* cumulatively determined direction has made possible.

Human utterance or judgment is thus co-extensive with all that is produced by the human process as such. A major historic misconception with respect to judgment is that it is necessarily deliberative. But human judging cannot be limited to occasions of intention or voluntary choice. It is the process wherein complexes which go to constitute the human creature perpetually impose upon him options. For the most part he cannot contemplate these; but owing to the duress of the world, he must selectively resolve the contrarieties they entail. Each instance of judging— though these instances are not to be regarded as neatly isolated —is at bottom an attitude or stance adopted. It is by his stances that a man, in so far as he can, determines and redetermines the complexes of his world. Each of his products is such a stance. It is a stand. He judges in so far as he exercises the selectiveness or discriminativeness inherent in his constitution; in so far as he actualizes the possibilities that lie in his accumulated traits. He judges continuously, through what he includes and excludes, preserves and destroys, is inclined to and averse to; through what he makes and fails to make, through the ways he acts and refrains from acting, through what he believes and disavows. His attitudes, and hence his commitments, are his whether he is aware of them or not.

To say that a man judges, for example, through what he makes, does not mean that he makes after he has discriminated and selected and become committed. It means that his making what he makes *is the way* he has discriminated and selected and become committed. The same applies to acting. When we ordinarily think of a stand or a commitment we tend to think of something dramatic: a heroic "stand," a "true" commitment. We overlook the minute stands, the small threads of utterance. These are the judgments that consist of the makings, sayings, and doings of everyday habit and impulse. In their collectivity and social efficacy, these threads of judgment are what determine the difference between a revolution and an abortive eruption, or between the firmness ˉof a tradition and the weakness of a tradition.

An adequate conception of judgment must avoid two other, corollary misconceptions which have dominated virtually the entire history of philosophy. One is the view that judging is a specific operation, an operation like remembering, abstracting, or attending (to cite the standard examples). Judging has never been linked with walking, talking, hearing, breathing, or eating; for it has been construed not merely as an "operation" but as a "mental" operation. Such a view cannot be defended by moralizing that we are dealing here with a word that has always been used in a certain way and there is no reason for it to be used in any other way. As a matter of fact, the uses of the word "judgment" have varied, and varied with considerable range—suggesting, for example, "presumption," "evaluation," "estimation," "decision," "discernment"—despite their misconception in common. The possible thought that the way a man is judging the world around him, or his fellow men, may not be present to his awareness, and that it is as a man that a man judges rather than in virtue of a special judging faculty or power that he possesses, seems never to have taken hold. This failure can be explained in terms of a number of stiff philosophical bulwarks that will doubtless endure forever. Let it suffice here to say that it reflects a simple but disastrous equation of selection with conscious selection, of discrimination with deliberate discrimination, of attitudinal postures with voluntarily chosen outlooks.

The second corollary misconception, as ancient and persistent as the first, is that human judgment always takes the form of thinking something or saying something about something else. When we are said to judge, it is supposed that we venture a truth claim; that we affirm a room to be fourteen feet wide, one umbrella to be better than another, some reforms to be viable and others not. This propositional conception of judgment requires that all judgments be regarded as either true or false, as more likely or less likely to be verified, as either in accordance with "the facts" ("the case") or not. It is a bias of intellectualism, and it is held, ironically enough, by the philosophers who decry intellectualism. Probably the bias stems from the Greek conviction that theoretical knowledge is the "highest" form of human attainment, above the attainments of social practice or of art. This conviction is bolstered by others. The theoretical, quite understandably, is identified with linguistic rendition or deliverance, and linguistic rendition with propositional or declarative communication. Though the Greek view of what is "highest" has often been abandoned, mainly on the basis of moral considerations, its effect on the concept of judgment has not.

The propositional conception of judgment and the conception of judgment as a mental operation sustain and perpetuate each other. The typical image of judging as requiring meditation, as requiring skill, as being something good to be able to do, as being something that we can suspend at will, and as culminating in the kind of expert authority exemplified by the judge on the bench, reflects the view of an intellective faculty that becomes developed professionally. And this image both fosters and is fed by the view of assertive language as the sharpest, the clearest, the most reliable, the most explicit, way of "expressing" ourselves, hence the only way of expertly judging. Thus the actual roots of judgment, which lie in the most basic dimensions of human functioning—in man's assimilation and manipulation of natural complexes—are obscured.

Human utterance is the net product of man and of men. It is

what emerges from the human order of judgment and particular orders within that order. It is not man's products reduced to propositions, a mistake which explains the widespread identification of utterance with linguistic utterance, even in the face of the fact that so much of language is not propositional at all. When the idea of utterance has been associated with man, and not merely this or that man, still another unfortunate transition has taken place: "utterance" has acquired a eulogistic import. But the tendency to think of human utterance as inherently good cannot be defended, any more than the tendency to think of man as inherently good. The products of men have been sometimes good and sometimes bad, and there is no way of separating utterance from its manifestations. Human utterance is manifested by concentration camps, bombs, and child beating along with agriculture, medicine, and poetry.

The bent of an individual's process of judging reflects the cumulative character of a human history. The varieties of judgment to be found in a perspectival order will depend both upon what has happened to him who is defined by the order, including the impact of judgments not his own, and upon what previous judgments have been his. Every judgment arises in an order of judgment, and orders of judgment arise in a human order, as motions arise in a mechanical order and chromosomes in a biological order. The conditions which give rise to particular judgments that have some degree of human importance—say to a sociological hypothesis, a poem, and a vote cast in an election— are located (they function) in the common area as it were of several orders. Thus each of these judgments (which all happen to be of the purposive or intended kind) is located in a social order, a psychological order, a historical order, an order of products (other judgments) customarily linked to science, art, and citizenship, and an order (subaltern to the preceding order) of products customarily linked to sociology, poetry, and political action. The various traits of a judgment are rooted in one or more of these ordinal locations. Some orders may provide determinants of a judgment's occurrence. Others may provide determinants of its meaning, its communicative efficacy. The meaning of some judgments may be articulated partly by ascertaining the circumstances of their origin. The meaning of others may be articulated only by ascertaining the role(s) which they play in their continuing relations, and ultimately in the relational complexes of communication. As a product, a judgment, whether intended or unintended, has effect. Like any other natural complex, its relations may be far-reaching or may prevail in a highly restricted domain.

Although there are many levels of judgment, and although judgment as such is inevitable and ubiquitous, it is imperative to understand the three principal modes into which it is divisible and in terms of which it is interpretable. Not that individual judgments always stand out clearly in practice. But the three modes of judgment are the essential ways in which human products *function*. A given complex produced by an individual without special foresight may, under appropriately different circumstances, function in all three ways. It is the differentiation, however, which is of greatest theoretical importance. (1) When we can be said to predicate, state, or affirm, by the use of words or by any other means; when the underlying direction is to achieve or support belief; when it is relevant to cite evidence in behalf of our product, we produce in the mode of assertive judgment, we judge assertively. (2) When we can be said to do or to act; when the underlying direction is toward effecting a result; when "bringing about" is the central trait attributable to our product, we produce in the mode of active judgment, we judge actively. (3) When we contrive or make, in so far as the contrivance rather than its role in action is what dominates and is of underlying concern; when the process of shaping and the product as shaped is central, we produce in the mode of exhibitive judgment, we judge exhibitively. On the methodic level, where (minimally) purposiveness and intention belong to judgments, assertive judgment is exemplified by science, or more generally, inquiry (including any discipline that makes a truth claim); active judgment, by deliberate conduct morally assessable; exhibitive judgment, by art.

Many everyday situations which are resignedly classified as perplexities and dilemmas are not without their possible explanation. But they cry out for theoretical clarification in a philosophic perspective. Often, for example, we cannot understand what it means for a man to "say one thing" and "do another." We explain in terms of moral indecision, emotional confusion, and the like. But we fail to realize that when one phase of conduct does not square with another, we may be oversimplifying the process of judgment involved. A man who does not act in accordance with what he says is not "lapsing from" or "betraying" a judgment he has made. He is judging in another way, judging actively. In terms of his prevailing makeup and direction, or in terms of circumstances that gain influence, his judgment in one mode is superseded by his judgment in another, whether for better or worse. It works the other way too. Active judgment may be superseded by assertive. Or both active and assertive judgment may be superseded by exhibitive. An artist may make the most irresponsible assertions about art, or about his own art. But the actual pursuit and exemplification of his art, his process of exhibitive judgment, may be the best index to his fundamental direction, and may be the best order in which his meanings are conveyed.

It is worth repeating that the three modes of utterance are to be understood in terms of the way in which human products actually function. Although we associate certain types of products habitually with some one of these functions, and may be entirely justified in doing so, there is no fixed type of product required for any mode of judging, and it is possible for one and the same product to function in any mode or combination of the modes, depending on the order in which it is located and the conditions prevailing in that order. We tend to think, for instance, of declarative sentences as the medium of assertion, and of bodily movement as the vehicle of action; but sentences can acquire the function of judging actively, and bodily movements the function of judging assertively. Take the economic product which consists in a private purchase of swamp land that has been known to be detrimental to public health. Ordinarily, we should think of this as an active judgment, with economic and social consequences appraisable in moral terms. If, however, the purchase occurs in the midst of controversy over the question whether private enterprise is more responsive to social need than government is, it may function as an assertive judgment which answers a standing question in the affirmative. But again, if the transaction functions as the beginning of a project to transform the swamp into landscaped terrain that is justified in terms of the transformation as such, it is an exhibitive judgment.

Treating the products of language as primarily assertive is a profound mistake. Language exemplifies an assertive function when it is propositional or intended as such. When language is poetic it is exhibitive in function. Language of whatever grammatical mood or emotional cast may actually function in any mode of judgment. The use of language to exhort, to arouse the performance of a deed, to bring about results—to function actively—is known by everybody to be as common as language used to affirm belief.

Often a product is oriented toward a function in one mode but actually functions in another. Political discourse, purporting to lay down verifiable contentions, to function assertively, may in intent or in effect or both, be a form of active judgment, determining a course of response. A medical technique practised in a large number of cases may be a recurrent form of active judgment, but in the order of general medical awareness the same technique practised may have an assertive function as bearing on the truth of a medical hypothesis.

All three of the modes of judgment may generate feeling, either in their producers or in others to whom their products are related. All three may entail feeling on other levels. A feeling may function as an event, a concomitant of judgment among other concomitants, like glandular activity and the weather. It may function as an aspect of judgment, perhaps a beginning, an incipient phase of judgment; or as the guiding tone whose relative intensity and fluctuations help to determine force of judgment and change of judgment.

The present approach is to be distinguished from one which would merely lay stress upon man as sayer, doer, and maker. That stress can acquire force not by reiterating itself as a tripartite classification—for such a classification has always been more or less available—but by insisting on the relevance of all three functions in any adequate account of the human process and its products. Historically, saying, doing, and making have all been recognized at least tacitly as essential foci for man. Saying, because of its association with speech, has always been regarded as most distinctively human. It has been regarded as representing "mind" and therefore as most fundamental in the characterization of knowledge, experience, meaning, and judgment. The force of the tripartite recognition is thus defeated, though not solely because the three functions are accorded unequal importance. It is defeated because it is unaccompanied by the realization that a judicative character belongs to all three. To assume that stating is alone judicative is to assume that it is the sole means by which man discriminates and appropriates traits of his world. Yet, merely to recognize, for example, that a work of art exhibits and doesn't have to state, is not enough. The main consideration is that the work is an exhibitive judgment. Otherwise we have provided no basis for a function comparable to stating, and the false implication is allowed that the work of art always conforms to the model of a dumb-show pointing to one-knows-not-what, or to the model of total sensory-affective involvement—both wholly noncommittal.

None of the three modes of judgment is intrinsically more fundamental than any of the others. But any may become more deserving of emphasis than the others in the circumstances of living. None of the modes is reducible to either of the others in the sense that what it produces can be arrived at or be more satisfactorily produced by the other, or in the sense that one is a special case of the other. In thus assuming the irreducibility of each mode and the parity of importance that obtains among the three, the question of "translation" arises. The principle of irreducibility would seem to preclude any mode being translatable into another and the other not being translatable into it. Can the modes, then, be translated into one another? The concept of translation, as we saw in the preceding chapter, is ambiguous. For the purpose of answering the question, we may formulate in the briefest terms a distinction which is of utmost importance. None of the modes is translatable *into* any other. Any of the modes is translatable *by* any other. In other words, if "translation" means "achieving an interchangeable equivalent," mutual translation of the modes is not possible. If "translation" means "articulating in another order of utterance," mutual translation is possible. The modes of judgment, though not reducible, are relatable, and often related in practice. Translation in the second, broader sense, as articulation or continuing exposure of a product's traits, extending the being of a product into a perspectival order made newly available, is the foundation of criticism, literary or any other kind. Even in this sense, it may not be desirable in all situations. But ideally, it permits us to see how the various facets of human invention can accent and augment one another in the interest of human betterment.

iii

Exhibitive judgment, exemplified on the methodic level by art, but in no way restricted to the commonly recognized arts, is the process whereby men shape natural complexes and communicate them for assimilation as thus shaped—as novel complexes distinguished from their bearing upon action and belief. To assimilate a novel complex exhibited *as* that complex does *not* imply im- response, or a response concerned with a "surface." On the con- mediate or unmediated response. Nor does it imply an all-or-none

trary, to a methodic exhibitive product, as to any other methodi-
cally wrought product of more than trivial significance, the only
kind of response that can be called human is one that, poten-
tially, continues and renews itself. The reason is that the meaning
of a judgment, in any of the three modes, is grasped only through
articulation of that judgment, and there is no foreseeable termi-
nus to the process of articulation. It is even more accurate to say
that the meaning of a judgment is *achieved* by articulation. The
usual way of describing the matter suggests that a meaning al-
ready obtains and is already present in the product. Actually the
meanings which already obtain have been transferred from sim-
ilar perspectives ("contexts"); they are preliminary and obvious,
and taken for granted as "there." There obviousness makes us
think of them as prior to articulation. But they are the result of
articulations that have become standardized. The product "has"
meaning. But being a judgment, it can have meaning only when
it means, that is, when its communicative function takes effect,
expands, and advances; when its role in a perspectival order is
determined and increasingly well determined. As the response to
artistic judgment must thus be considered to be the beginning of
a process of response, so must the satisfaction attending that re-
sponse. Being satisfied, like perceiving and like understanding,
is not an all-or-none result, is not attained all at once, and is not
limited to single occasions of responding.

A poem, or work of poetry in whatever form, is an exhibitive
judgment wrought in language. We may speak of exhibitive
judgments within the poem. And we may speak of a sequence of
poems, or an entire body of poetry, as an exhibitive judgment of
greater sweep, multifariously constituted. As a linguistic contriv-
ance, a poem must be distinguished from non-poetic forms of
literature. But initially we must think of it in the way we may
think of all literature, as exemplifying a non-assertive mode of
discriminating natural complexes, a mode which is itself diversi-
fied and continuingly defined by the range of literary products.

Here it will be desirable to pause, in order to comment upon a fundamental terminological usage which has thus far been given no formal attention. The expression "natural complex" (which we have been abbreviating as "complex") applies to whatever is, and therefore to whatever can be dealt with; to what is produced by men as well as to what is not. It is the expression we have been using for whatever we wish to include in our range of reference without having to specify a mode of being. The term "natural" is important, not as a qualification used in order to concede that some complexes can be "non-natural," but on the contrary as a reminder that *all* complexes are aspects of nature; that no complex can be dismissed or exorcised. Closely related to this usage is the conception of ontological parity, already alluded to and shortly to be dealt with in greater detail. In "natural complex" we are thus provided with a category (or more strictly, a pre-categorial device) by means of which a subject can be brought to a sphere of discussion in the most general terms possible. Such a category has advantages over others which have been relied upon traditionally to subserve a general encompassment prior to specification. It is much less naïve, much less ambiguous than "thing" ("all the things that poetry can deal with") which always threatens to limit our scope by its suggestion of a space-time particular as the basic model. And it is much less awkward than "entity" or "being" or "object." "Natural complex" enables us to talk of whatever it is that poetry may be concerned with and to include in the "whatever" not only public space-time particulars but any kind of actualities—actual parts of animals, actual traits of an illusion, actual revolutionary ideas, actual components of a dream; and any kind of possibilities— possible parts of animals and possible relations of men, possibilities of awareness, transformation, comparison, fulfillment and tragic defeat, life and death. To refer to what may become identified as a possibility of transformation by the term "an entity," or "a being," or "an object," at once assimilates it to the model of a "substance" or an individual. To refer to it as a natural complex involves no covert special model and no prior ontological classification. All that the term suggests at first blush is potential diversity and manyness within the unity of its reference. The use of the term does indeed reflect a definite metaphysical orientation. It eliminates the idea that what we are concerned with can be regarded as "non-natural," as intrinsically and necessarily discontinuous with any of the possibilities or actualities of the world, as other than a nature of some kind, whether produced or not produced by man. It also eliminates the idea that there are or that we may be concerned with "simples." The simple, the seamless, the absolutely pure and non-complex, is in effect the traitless. To assume that any "what" or "that" is simple is to assume that it has no diversity of traits and therefore no trait in common with any other "that"; it has only the trait which constitutes its difference from all others. Thus it is without relational traits, and is unlocated in the world. A simple could not be.

We return to the general theme of poetry as a form of exhibitive judgment. Taken historically, in reaction to the misunderstanding of poetic utterance, Sidney's principle that the poet "nothing affirms, and therefore never lieth" is remarkably sound. To go on to say as he does that the poet "never affirmeth" is equivocal; the words should be read to mean "never affirmeth as poet." For actually there are poets, and perhaps many, who do seek to affirm without bothering about the interpretation of their procedure; and surely there is no reason for them to bother. There are even poets who seek to affirm that their art affirms.

> Why take the artistic way to prove so much?
> Because, it is the glory and good of Art
> That Art remains the one way possible
> Of speaking truth, to mouths like mine at least.

And then, as if by way of qualification,

> But Art,—wherein man nowise speaks to men,
> Only to mankind,—Art may tell a truth
> Obliquely, do the thing shall breed the thought,
> Nor wrong the thought, missing the mediate word.[1]

It is enough to say that assertive judgments may occur in poetry but are extrinsic to it, in the sense that they are not essential, not common, and not pursued with respect to assertive validation. The mere presence of what appear to be declarative statements in poetry is deceptive. We tend to think that the grammatical mood of the words is the key to their function—a carryover from the forms of everyday discourse, which are themselves no reliable index of function. But in any event, an assertive component of a poem does not make the poem assertive. In poetic drama assertions are definitely made by the characters. But the drama as such is exhibitive judgment, and so are the characters' assertions considered as poetic speech. The tissue of (assertive) argumentation, of consecutiveness and persuasiveness, that is often to be found in poetry (dramatic or other) is the strategic means (sometimes precisely because it is the most familiar means) by which a complex of traits is encompassed and bound together, integrated as an exhibitive structure. Nothing could be as irrelevant to such a structure, as incongruous with it, as the question of its inferential validity. Similarly misleading is that species of grammatical declarativeness to be found in the "descriptive" form or style of much poetry. Poetic description is not assertion. No one is significantly engaged by the issue of whether such a description is accurate, adequate, or appropriate; and no one is disposed to find out whether the inferential musings in which it is immersed are conclusive or inconclusive.

> The long triumphant nose attains—retains
> Just the perfection; and there's scarlet-skein
> My ancient enemy, her lip and lip,
> Sense-free, sense-frighting lips clenched cold and bold
> Because of chin, that based resolve beneath!
> Then the columnar neck completes the whole
> Greek-sculpture-baffling body! Do I see?
> Can I observe? You wait next word to come?
> Well, wait and want! since no one blight I bid
> Consume one least perfection. Each and all,
> As they are rightly shocking now to me,

So may they still continue! Value them?
Ay, as the vendor knows the money-worth
Of his Greek statue, fools aspire to buy,
And he to see the back of! Let us laugh!
You have absolved me from my sin at least!
You stand stout, strong, in the rude health of hate,
No touch of the tame timid nullity
My cowardice, forsooth, has practised on! [2]

The poetic description cannot be appraised as right or wrong, or even as good or bad, for though it presupposes certain standards of verbal meaning, it presupposes no measure of credibility or propriety. The passage just quoted is a segment of a more comprehensive exhibitive judgment which frames a contour of traits, including visual appearances, sharp feelings, submerged attitudes, and links to antiquity. It is a process of definition, marking out an area of relatedness, plotting boundaries (in a human complex), as when we define a parcel of land or define the course of travel. In this sense all shaping, all contriving, all art, entails a process of defining. And in this sense removed to a deeper level, every actuality limits and bounds other actualities, partly defines their scope. The process of defining is thus not restricted to, and sometimes does not fit, the familiar procedure of arriving at formulae of usage designed to be recurrently applicable. It may aim at establishing an integrity for a complex not hitherto possessed (judged) by us, yet related to complexes in our ken. Poetic description is one of the forms of poetic definition, and poetic definition is one of the forms of exhibitive definition. Poetically, the following lines (composed, in the original, about four thousand years ago) are a description in the very same sense as the lines just quoted.

Death is in my eyes today
As when a sick man becomes whole,
As when one walketh abroad after sickness.

Death is in my eyes today
Like the scent of myrrh;
As when one sitteth under the boat's sail on a windy day.

Death is in my eyes today
Like the smell of water-lilies;
As when one sitteth on the bank of drunkenness.

Death is in my eyes today
Like a well-trodden road,
As when one returneth from the war unto his home.

Death is in my eyes today
Like the unveiling of heaven
As when one attaineth to that which he knew not.

Death is in my eyes today
As when one longeth to see his house again
After he hath spent many years in captivity.[3]

These considerations may help us to see where Coleridge goes astray in thinking of certain types of poetry (like *The Ancient Mariner*) as requiring the reader to achieve "that willing suspension of disbelief for the moment, which constitutes poetic faith." For poetry of any kind, the suspension of disbelief is no more prerequisite than the suspension of belief. In general, belief and disbelief cannot be simply suspended; they cannot be provisionally undone by a personal resolution. Conviction is not dissolved and rebuilt gratuitously. The very idea is self-contradictory. Faith is not worth much if it can be set up and removed like an ornament on a mantel-piece. But in particular, the mode of poetic response is not a matter of belief at all. The traditional apologetic attitude in behalf of poetry, and the traditional condescension toward it, alike reflect the deficiency in the age-old version of judgment.

We have said that the three modes of judgment, though not reducible to any one of them, are mutually articulatable. Assertive judgments may be articulated actively or exhibitively, active judgments articulated assertively or exhibitively, exhibitive judgments articulated assertively or actively. For example, a social reform movement may, through its action, articulate a social theory. The articulation may proceed in the other direction: social thought about the nature of human institutions may articulate historical chains of action. In the same way poetry may exhibitively articulate a trend of ideation, such as a philosophic system or a general intellectual movement. In so doing it represents such a trend without becoming involved in evidential considerations. Like all articulative judgment, it extends the being of a product by a new perspectival determination of that product's traits. It defines the product's character in another order of human concern. Once again, the articulation may move in the opposite direction as well. A philosophic outlook may articulate propositionally what it finds in poetic utterance. How poetry can articulate products within its own order of judgment; how it can exhibitively probe a method, a life, a temperament, another poetic product, is profoundly conveyed by the lines of Shelley on Coleridge which Arthur Symons quotes to show the power of the poet as critic.[4]

> You will see Coleridge—he who sits obscure
> In the exceeding lustre and the pure
> Intense irradiation of a mind,
> Which, with its own internal lightning blind,
> Flags wearily through darkness and despair—
> A cloud-encircled meteor of the air,
> A hooded eagle among blinking owls.[5]

Literary criticism may find that the character of a given poetic work reflects an ideational scheme or tradition by which it has been influenced. In articulating that scheme, the critic articulates the poetry. But not infrequently, his mistake is to think of the poetry itself as asserting the scheme. Whitehead, in his use of Milton, Pope, Wordsworth, Shelley, and Tennyson to express the historical opposition of mechanism and organicism, helps to illustrate certain articulative aspects of their poetry. As he sees the matter, however, the broad scale on which their longer poems are projected "gives [the poems] a didactic character." This way of approaching poetry and the poetic articulation of philosophic thought runs into serious trouble. We soon find Whitehead condemning Tennyson's *In Memoriam* for avoiding the "problem" of "individual moral responsibility" while dealing with virtually every other "religious and scientific problem." He even concludes that "the enfeeblement of thought in the modern world is illustrated by the way in which this plain issue is avoided in Tennyson's poem." [6] However we may feel about a particular poem, or whatever function its author may have considered himself to be performing, it is a monstrous distortion to think of poetry in terms of philosophic completeness and adequacy, of argumentative cogency, or of problem-solving. Whitehead ultimately obscures the nature of poetic articulation for want of a distinction between assertive and exhibitive judgment.

iv

It should be increasingly clear that the theory of judgment needs to introduce a category that will help us understand the *exploratory* character which may belong to any type of judgments on the methodic level, and therefore to poetry. Traditionally, it is to science as inquiry, credible investigation of the world, and to philosophy construed as aspiring to scientific status, that the trait of "seriousness" is ascribed. The linguistic nature of poetry in virtue of which it has so often been thought pre-eminent among the arts, has also been the very basis of its disparagement in contrast to science: what can poetic language "say" if poetry is not inquiry? Hence, alternatively, the easy identification of poetry with play, frivolity, "fancy" or the unrestricted toleration of images, and linguistic self-indulgence. This identification cannot be combated by making poetry quasi-assertive. Poetry's exploratory character is of a different breed.

The first step in formulating this character is to determine the genus we need. Inquiry must be regarded as only one species of Query. Art is another. The art of poetry is another—a sub-species. All exemplify the interrogative temper. In poetry this does not entail asking a question and looking for an answer. In science it not only does, but further entails both the initial sep-aration of questions and their structuring. For these questions do more than raise the hope of unequivocal answers; they guide the process of achieving them. When the ancient Greeks said that the pursuit of wisdom begins in wonder, they laid the foundation for the concept of query. But there are at least two kinds of won-der. There is the wonder that seeks to be appeased and the won-der to which appeasement is irrelevant. In the species of query exemplified by science, the former dominates; in that exemplified by poetry, the latter. Scientific wonder seeks to resolve the ques-tions it provokes. Poetic wonder seeks no resolutions; its inter-rogativeness is not generated by vexations.[7] Each of these forms of query methodically discriminates traits in the world. Each com-bines, separates, juxtaposes, varies the configurations and frames of, traits. Initially, science finds the traits to be problematical, po-tentially if not actually. Initially, poetry finds them to be just what it finds them to be. Terminally, a scientific *finding* excludes and opposes other findings previously thought to be possible. Termi-nally, a poetic *finding* opposes no others. Yet it is the finding that it is, and not another. Scientific wonder, despite its need for mitigation, extends itself systematically. Poetic wonder seeks its own extension, though each poetic product inevitably curbs itself as a contrivance, in order to be a contrivance at all. A scientific product eventually aims to relate to another as an explanatory whole of which the other is an evidential or implied part, or as a part of the other. A poetic product does not aim at such a rela-tion. In saying that a poetic finding "opposes" no others, or that a poetic product does not "aim" at the kind of relation with an-other which obtains between scientific products, the reference is to the finding as finding, the product as product; to the nature of the product as a judgment. What a particular poet's motives are, what aims he may have to "oppose" or discredit some poetic trend that he deplores, is beside the point. No poem as such opposes any other poem, because all poems may co-exist as independently justifiable manifestations of query, and none can be meaningfully "invalidated" by any other.

The interrogative temper of poetry, like that of science and other species of query, lies in its seeking. Its seeking and its finding are less easily distinguishable than those of science. Poetic wonder, accepted on its own account, adds to the store of wonder. This does not mean that the poetic stance as such is committed to admiration of the world's complexes. Even the formal poetic encomium exemplifies query in so far as it is poetry, and not necessarily in so far as it is an encomium. What poetry selects as its elements of contrivance attests its infinitely variable interests. What provides for these interests a poetic direction is not the kind of complex selected but the mode of judgment embodied.

The concept of exhibitive judgment makes it possible to avoid two untenable extremes of opinion. One is that poetry has its own kind of claim to truth, implicitly if not explicitly. The other is that poetry need not be construed as utterance at all—a view which, expectedly or unexpectedly, is suggested by Archibald MacLeish's line "A poem should not mean but be," when this line is extracted (as it has been) to serve as a piece of criticism. The first of these extremes is much less confident of itself when confronted by the questions what constitutes poetic falsification, how poems can be said to oppose one another with conflicting claims, and whether and how such claims can be settled. A charitable interpretation of the second extreme is that it identifies the meaning of all products with assertive meaning, and hence understandably repudiates meaning so far as poetry is concerned. In so far as it emphasizes a poem as something that simply "is," it obliterates the difference between (poetic) products and mere (unproduced) events. Yet events too can have meaning, when present in a perspective that becomes articulated through judgment. The repudiation of a narrow and unjust conception of meaning can easily fall into stultifying despair, with its own dogmatic conviction that no conception of meaning can possibly be adequate to poetry. The pessimism is exacerbated by other widely held assumptions about meaning—the assumption that if artistic meaning is incomplete, or gets expanded as time goes on, it is necessarily cloudy or arbitrary to begin with; or the assumption that scientific meanings are complete and wholly determinate; or the assumption that a meaning must be unequivocal and determinate in order to be a meaning at all. That a scientific meaning cannot ever be deemed complete is clear from the simple logical consideration that there is no end to the number of consequences entailed by a proposition, and that therefore the burden of all the assertions latent in a proposition of science cannot be known at any given time. Different dimensions of scientific meaning lie in the relations which a scientific product can bear to previous and subsequent scientific products—such as logical and historical relations—not to mention other products generally, and other conditions of the physical or social world. To suppose a scientific meaning complete, fixed, and unequivocal in the midst of so many possible changes and perspectives is not merely to hold a dubious metaphysics but to ignore the history of science. About artistic meaning we puzzle ourselves no end, but less because of its kind of intricacy or because of our prior doubts about the artistic enterprise than because in our comparisons of art with everyday meaning we overestimate the constancy and availability of the latter. All meaning is achieved by the process of judicative articulation, and it is a serious error to regard this process as ever actually completed except in the sense that we have chosen to stop it. To think that an equivocal meaning is no meaning at all is very much like thinking that an undeveloped economy is no economy at all or a perplexed person no person at all.

Seeing poetry in terms of the interrogative temper demands some caution, lest the seeing be too narrowly focussed. (1) Poetry does not need to introduce the grammatical appearance, or the suggestion, of verbal questioning in order to be interrogative—in order to exemplify the process of query. Nor is it enough to say that the words shaped as a question in poetry need not and do not aim to be answered.

> My face in thine eye, thine in mine appeares,
> And true plain hearts doe in the faces rest,
> Where can we finde two better hemispheares
> Without sharpe North, without declining West? [8]

Grammatically shaped questions are not what is *relevant* to the exploratory genius of poetry.

(2) The interrogative temper of poetry does not eliminate or transcend meaning. Meaning is not superseded by shaping but rather given its character as meaning in an order of exhibitive judgment.

The point of these two observations will be evident if we glance at a passage from Sartre's *What Is Literature?* Apart from the dubious emphasis we are using it to illustrate, it is a fine passage. It starts by quoting two lines from Rimbaud:

> Oh seasons! Oh castles!
> What soul is faultless?
>
> (*O saisons! O châteaux!*
> *Quelle âme est sans défaut?*)

And it goes on to say:

Nobody is questioned; nobody is questioning; the poet is absent. And the question involves no answer, or rather is its own answer. Is it therefore a false question? But it would be absurd to believe that Rimbaud "meant" that everybody has his faults. As Breton said of Saint-Pol Roux, "If he had meant it, he would have said it." Nor did he *mean* to say something else. He asked an absolute question. He conferred upon the beautiful word "soul" an interrogative existence. The interrogation has become a thing as the anguish of Tintoretto became a yellow sky. It is no longer a signification, but a substance.[9]

(1) Rimbaud certainly produced "an interrogative existence." But just as certainly, it is not upon the word "soul" alone that he conferred such an existence. All the poetry of Rimbaud, all poetry, is interrogative in its process of probing and in the radiation of wonder. All poets communicate the interrogative strain, even those whose manner is categorical, and those in whom we find a verbal order that seems to incarnate assertiveness.

> Thus God and Nature link'd the general frame,
> And bade self-love and social be the same.[10]

Pope is not a theologian, a moral theorist, a practical moralist, a historian of ideas, or a logician. We do not admire in him or in any other poet theoretical power or rigorous reasoning. Whether the grammatical garments he employs are those of satire, description, approbation, or demonstration, it is the complex of traits he has set before us as shaped that emerges, essential and indomitable, from query. The very same exhibitive process is going on when Pope employs the actual grammatical form of asking a question and of answering it.

> Who starves by nobles, or with nobles eats?
> The wretch that trusts them, and the rogue that cheats.[11]

What scientists, statesmen, philosophers, or revolutionists bring into the world is probed by the poet even as clouds, hopes, dreams, flowers, and love are; so that his subject as it appears poetically may appear in the shape of a doctrine, a conclusion, a social movement, a commentary. The issue of whether he is moralist or poet is settled not by what complexes he has chosen, or what titles he has given to his works; not by his decision, but by his mode of production. In poetry, as we have seen, even a body of assertions is not dealt with assertively. The exhibitive judgment of the poet, his mode of selection, control, and discrimination, moulds a body of traits, and the moulding may have been kindled by an assertion that he has encountered. The exhibitive discrimination of the assertive—of concepts, controversies, doctrines—is the re-discrimination of a complex. The concepts and doctrines are spirited into another order, relocated by the force of query.

> Mock on, mock on, Voltaire, Rousseau;
> Mock on, mock on; 'tis all in vain!
> You throw the sand against the wind,
> And the wind throws it back again.
>
> And every sand becomes a gem
> Reflected in the beams divine;
> Blown back they blind the mocking eye
> But still in Israel's paths they shine.
>
> The Atoms of Democritus
> And Newton's Particles of Light
> Are sands upon the Red Sea shore
> Where Israel's tents do shine so bright.[12]

(2) The word become "substance" or "thing" does not cease to mean just because it is no longer exclusively verbal. Sartre thinks that, being a "substance," it is "no longer a signification." But a word or phrase never does signify or mean solely because it is verbal, or because it was once tied to a discriminandum. It signifies because it enters into a communicative function. Any natural complex can be appropriated for a communicative function. A word or other complex to which no independent "signification" can be attributed, yet has significance. The word that has become "more" than a word has meaning (it means) in virtue of the same process by which the word as such had meaning—in so far as its ordinal habitat and function have been articulated. And we must be clear that the interrogativeness of a poem or of its words is no special achievement of a particular poet. The poem as poem

arouses further query—through its articulation in the form of criticism, through its articulation (exhibitive and active) by other poems of the same tradition or movement, or through its cultivation of the desire for poetry. It arouses query through its contagion of seeking, in any mode, any medium, any degree.

VI

ONTOLOGICAL PARITY
AND THE SENSE OF
PREVALENCE

i

Having identified poetry as a form of query which is embodied in exhibitive judgment of a linguistic character, we have mapped, as it were, the area for the discovery of attributes that will distinguish poetry most sharply from non-poetic forms of literary art.

Those who have thought of poetry in terms of its delineative power have sometimes tried to assimilate it to painting. The parallel between the two arts, drawn since Greek and Roman antiquity, became more developed but also more problematical with the passage of time. Those who have thought of poetry in terms of its sonance have tried to assimilate it to music. Classically, music was most often but not always regarded as ancillary to it.[1] In recent opinion, the relation between poetry and music is suggested by the relation between poetry and speech. The emphasis upon speech as such can be pushed only so far, for prose of all kinds also is spoken. Poetic speech, after all, reflects poetic language: the character of poetic speech rests upon the words that determine how such speech will sound. But it should not be assumed that there is a portion of poetic language specifically relevant to its sound—alliteration, rhyme, assonance. All the words in poetry are relevant to its sound. Specific techniques or devices only contribute types of sound the properties of which are more or less known in advance. But the individual words and word-configurations, the spoken phrases and sequences, the rhythm decisions, do not yet constitute all the determinants of poetic sound. The meaning of individual words and the import of the general word order affect the way sound is heard. Different imputed meanings as well as meaning anticipations provide conditions for sensory impact, somewhat as darkness and daylight differently affect the way we hear wildlife in the forest. Diction and sound are theoretically distinguishable but are not separable in the linguistic texture of spoken poetry. The essential communicative effect and the psychology of the reader addressed jointly determine the value of poetic speech. The meanings that emerge from poetry dictate the strategies of speaking (including the private speech of the reader), and the strategies of speaking affect the sound of what is spoken.

It should be possible now to see that the parallel so often drawn between poetic speech and music is a precarious one. The sonance of poetry is compounded of the several factors mentioned. It is no more actually music than poetic portrayal is painting with chemical materials. In a sense it is "analogous" to music, but this too is misleading, for music need not be associated with words, whereas the sound of poetic speech cannot be independent of words and their communicative effect. The expression "the music of poetry" seems to function, and even to be intended, as a panegyric, to the effect that the sound of poetry may be good enough to be regarded as music. That this type of panegyric is seldom thought out is indicated by the forms it is inclined to take. Its standard is not music as such, music of any kind, but a predetermined image of sonority or delight, such as the deep reverberations of a pipe organ and the vocal patterns of a madrigal. Highly dissonant music, predominantly percussive music, or hot jazz, is seldom associated with "the music of poetry." In one recent analysis, we find attributed to the language of poetry, merely as poetry, not just musicality but a "fulness" which is thought of as symphonic and is on this basis contrasted with most human language, which is said to be like the "thin pipings" of a pair of flutes. A question that should not be ignored in this connection is whether the sonant aspect of poetry—wholly aside from its identification with music—has ever been the most important aspect in poetry of the highest rank, the aspect in terms of which the poetry is thus ranked. It seems doubtful that it ever has been. This is not denied by Coleridge's "The man that hath not music in his soul can indeed never be a genuine poet." His stress is on the indispensability of the unlearned gift which consists in being sensitive to the sounds of words; his stress is not on the poetic primacy of this gift.

There is something unusually naïve in the idea of Poe and others that because poetry cannot be divorced from sound, it is necessarily musical. Sound as such, even rhythmic sound, is scarcely a sufficient condition of music. Equally naïve is the view that "the properties in which music concerns the poet most nearly are the sense of rhythm and the sense of structure" (T. S. Eliot).[2] Rhythm and structure pervade the universe and are ubiquitous in the life of man. The kinds of rhythm and structure that are distinctive of poetry do not have to be imported from outside the domain of speech and do not have to depend upon music. Whoever wishes to build linguistic rhythms on non-linguistic models can utilize an infinitude of sources, some as near as the patter of rain, breathing, geometrical forms, and the beating of the heart. To no one source is the poet tied, on none is he wholly dependent.

Can speech not be credited with subtleties of sound peculiar to itself? Must poetic speech in particular be conceived either in terms of its phonetic atoms or in terms of music? The sound of music and the sound of language are equally primordial and equally original. They have traits in common, but neither can be absorbed by the other. To inflate one art into two, or contract two arts into one, has a destructive side. Perhaps a latent sus-

picion of the danger accounts for Santayana speaking of poetry
as "subdued music." But the sound-complexes of poetry can be
justified for what they are, without being reduced to music or
defined by musical criteria.

The historical tendency to link poetry and *song* is especially
significant, because it persists regardless of the *way* in which the
relation is understood: poetry itself construed as song, poetry as
converted into song, poetry as enhanced by song. Culturally the
association is encouraged. Bard, troubadour, and minstrel are
nostalgic symbols of the poetic art voiced. A fair number of
poems in the modern period are called songs and odes. If we
allow ourselves to abstract from the cultural aspects of the older
tradition, we are obliged to ask both why such a tradition was
vigorous and why poetry and song should be associated at all.
We cannot explain by merely appealing to the attractiveness of
a social style, or to the inherent attractiveness of the combina-
tion. For the custom and the present-day impulse still is to refer
to the poet as a singer even though he no longer sings in the
sense of adhering to a musical discipline.

Better light on the meaning of the association may be intro-
duced by considering what takes place in the oral reading of
poetry. The reading of poetry differs from that of prose in its
inclination toward formality and solemnity. Many poets chant
or declaim in the reading of their work. "Solemnity" implies
nothing funereal. It implies a controlled intensity, a restrained
severity of manner. This manner is equally evident in the reading
of whimsical, comic, or satiric poetry. To a certain extent it re-
flects the need to preserve a metrical structure by means of styl-
ized vocal stress and cadence. But the same impulse, expressed by
the same species of formality, is present in the reading of non-
metrical poetry with appropriately different means of stress. It is
a common experience that where we have a body of words in
paragraph form, a decision to construe it as poetry rather than
prose will cause it to be read with a formalized cadence not pri-
marily in accord with the grammatical punctuation. Poetry may

be present in any literary form, and "prose poems" have been written by poets. But the need to preserve solemnity in the cadences is underscored by the fact that the great majority of poets, no matter how radical their viewpoint or their procedure, cling to a physical form which distinguishes their work from the conventional appearance of prose. The lines, for example, may each contain a large number of words, but they remain individualized and are not merged into a paragraph. Or the entire poem may form a printed geometric pattern, but the abandonment of the prose pattern is made conspicuous.

The solemnity of poetic speech sometimes seems to be taken as ceremonial or ritual in character. This is unfortunate: in a sense it evades the force of the next question that has to be asked, namely, What accounts for the tendency toward formality or solemnity? For we would need to ask also why the solemnity should assume the form of ceremony and ritual. These imply social practice, and periodicity as well. The oral communication of poetry, like poetry in general, is independent of such conditions. Except by the circumstance of voluntary agreement, it is tied to no institutional, tribal, or professional substratum. Neither does its peculiar kind of formality and intensity necessarily reflect the presence of a heavier weight of emotion. The weight of emotion in the prose of a political harangue or a memorial address may be at least as great. The impulse toward solemnity and its various manifestations—song, declamation, the stylized use of the voice—must reflect not primarily a communal commitment but an essential aspect of the poetic stance and its language. In other words, it is difficult to avoid the conclusion that the distinctive compulsion of poetic speech signifies something basic in poetic judgment.

Poetic judgment dictates the atmosphere of poetic speech. Poetic speech, by differentiating itself from other forms of speech, proclaims not a total removal from them but a transition to another mode of utterance. The elemental solemnity is the indication, the warning, and the reminder that we are in a unique state of query. Yet once again, the deliberateness of poetic speech does not imply that "a poem is a rite" (W. H. Auden).[3] This would confuse the symptom of poetic judgment with the poetic judgment. But neither is the symptom itself a ritual symptom; it is the evidence of poetic judgment unfolding. If the transition from the prose attitude to the poetic attitude involves a rite, then so does the transition from ordinary thinking to chemistry or mathematics or architecture, each of which requires a procedural and stylistic reorientation of a comparable kind. We cannot regard every methodic practice and every shift in awareness as ritual.

In signifying by vocal means the departure from both the "ordinary" or "everyday" level and the methodic prose level of language and of awareness, poetic speech enacts a transition from a hybrid or miscellaneously constituted order of judgment to the exhibitive mode. But a departure from ordinary speech is not necessarily a departure from ordinary words. Casual conversation and every conceivable familiar style can be utilized as the textural medium, even as the rhetoric of science or theology can. It is usually in the perspective occupied by ordinary speech that poetry is thought to be "indirect" and "oblique." Scientific discourse is not thought to be indirect or oblique, perhaps because it is seen primarily in its technological aspects, which are supposed to be universally intelligible. The impression of obliqueness derives partly from an oversimplified view of the artistic functions of language. (It derives mainly from an oversimplified view of language. The tradition still is to think of language as basically either "informative" or "emotive." What is typically classified as informative usually is a manifestation of assertive judgment. What is typically classified as emotive can manifest any mode of judgment, depending upon the communicative circumstances.) At first there seems to be a paradox here: why should the exhibitive dimension of language be regarded as oblique and the assertive dimension as direct? Should not "showing" be more direct than "telling"? We have warned against confusing exhibitive judgment with mere "exhibiting." Exhibitive judgment minimally implies a selective attitudinal process and product. Exhibitive judgment in the arts implies methodic discrimination and hence purposive contrivance: the showing is never a simple mirroring. Precisely the same principle applies to assertive judgment: the telling is not to be thought of in terms of pre-established grammatical and rhetorical forms. To uncritical awareness assertion is more direct only because it is associated with expected *moulds* of telling. The novel in its traditional narrative forms is regarded as more direct than poetry because, though it is also exhibitive, it is exhibitive in the (expected) guise of telling, "telling a story." The exhibitive language of poetry is deemed remote because it need not (and so often does not) assume this guise, and because it does not fit the kind of visual paradigm commonly associated with "showing."

Now in saying that poetic speech departs from the order or *perspective* to which everyday language and the prose habit are native, much more is implied than a change in mode of judgment, or in the linguistic manner consequent upon such a change in mode. The perspective abandoned is one that is dominated by a type of metaphysical disposition so deep-seated that it is invisible, an age-old outlook perpetuated in theoretical terms by most of the major figures in Western philosophy. According to this outlook, the ruling principle of which is a principle of ontological priority, man is provided by "the nature of things" with an unshakable basis for the guidance of his awareness and the preservation of his stability. This basis, regarded as a norm or absolute measuring-rod of "being," is most frequently called "reality." (Sometimes, in a more restricted expression that tends to divide philosophers who otherwise are uncritically committed to the general outlook, it is called "hard fact" or "the facts.") Human creatures are taught early, both by the circumstances of their personal life and by the normative influences of their culture, especially in its religious phase, to distinguish between "realities" and "appearances." Appearances are the deceptive, ephemeral,

unreliable complexes; realities, the permanent, inevitable, contin-
uous, recurrent, or coherent complexes. The realities are thought
of as basic to this world or to a promised world, or both. It does
not follow, of course, that the realities are better understood than
the appearances; nor is it often suspected that an appearance in
one circumstance may be a reality in another, and vice versa.[4] Phi-
losophers, less concerned than men of affairs with making their
world manageable and more with making it intelligible, develop
types of trust and distrust comparable to those of common life.
Some aspects of their world provide them with clues to other as-
pects. Some provide them with the impetus to build their guiding
concepts. Those which they are compelled repeatedly to acknowl-
edge, those to which they feel they are led back irresistibly in their
interpretations, get accredited as "real" or "most real." Degree of
explanatory usefulness gets transformed into degree of "being."
In more than one major philosophic tradition the very task of
philosophy is held to be a quest not merely for "reality" but for
"ultimate reality." The everyday distinction between trust-
worthy realities and deceptive appearances freezes into the
distinction between Reality and Appearance. The vague distinc-
tion between "things" that are "substantial" and the properties
that "belong" to them becomes the distinction between Primary
and Secondary being. Societies thus come to be held less real than
individuals, though (as we would expect where the *principle* of
ontological priority is accepted by both of the opposing sides)
individuals can come to be held less real than societies. Societies
are less real because they are "composed" of individuals; in-
dividuals are less real because they are "abstracted" from es-
sential wholes. Possibilities are held less real than actualities,
relations less real than the "things" related—blissfully disregard-
ing the consideration that every actuality has its possibilities
and could not "be" without any, and that every "thing" has its
relations, without which it could not be. There is "really" no per-
manence, only change. There is "really" no change, only per-
manence. Forms alone are real and abide, particular things are

transitory shadows. Particular things alone are real, forms are verbal fictions.

The literary term "fiction" reflects such a belief in ontological priority. Hence: a literary product, unlike an account given by history or journalism, is not an account of "real" life. Or: a literary product "imitates" or "represents" real life but is not part of it. Or: a literary product may talk about what is "real" but not about what is "actual." The literary product that can be bought, sold, or burned is acknowledged as "physically" real. Its communicative content is left ontologically dubious. The consideration that "fiction" can have and has had as great an effective impact on civilization and thought as "real happenings" is held to be mysterious. The reality of the impact remains unreconciled with the "unreality" of the story or *mythos*. Critical literary opinion, torn between adherence to the principle dictating a difference between real and unreal, and the troublesome need to explain the practice of poetry, is laden with a variety of awkward positions on the relation between poetry and "reality": poetry is an "imaginative" realm apart from reality; an imaginative "discovery" of reality; a way of "transcending" reality; a way of attaining a "higher" reality; and (most absurd of all) a way of "making reality more real."

The unique intonational impulse of poetic speech symbolizes its departure from the outlook of ontological priority to which ordinary speech is enslaved. (It symbolizes far more, as the next section will show.) Poetry as such, the poetic attitude and its language, simply ignores, disregards, this outlook. It does not affirm the disregard, it disregards. Whatever individual poets may believe, or believe they believe, their poetry imposes upon them an acceptance of all complexes as "there," as complexes to be dealt with, no matter in what way they are named or categorized. For whatever poetry discriminates (shapes, contrives), it recognizes and will not dismiss. *Whatever* it finds and makes is real, real enough to be found and made—or more exactly, neither more nor less real than either the conventionally identified realities or those realities deemed ontologically primary. All appearances are realities for the poet: his candor perceives that the mirage is a reality even as the pond is. It is necessary for us only to understand that although every discriminandum is as real as every other, not every one belongs to the same order as every other. The desert mirage belongs to a visual order, not to an order in which thirst is quenched. The pond may belong to both orders of being. The stick bent in water is really bent—in water, and as seen in water, not as touched. The railroad tracks do meet—but in the order of vision, not in the order of public space. Some complexes may have more or less importance, more or less prevasiveness, more or less moral significance, more or less interest, for the poet; but none has more or less being than any other. The poet's working attitude is an acceptance of ontological parity. "Acceptance" is the term rather than "assumption." Ontological parity does not function for the poet as a theoretical commitment or assertive presupposition. It functions as an unwillingness to deny the integrity of any complex discriminated. It is therefore an unwillingness to deny the reality of what is contrived, to think of what is humanly produced as secondary in being to what is not humanly produced. Acceptance in this sense is an active judgment relating to the pursuit of exhibitive judgment.

With the acceptance of ontological parity, the poet's power of query (his "imagination") is uninhibited. Poetic query is one of the ways in which traits are explored by human beings. All traits are equally traits, no matter how they are explored or how they are reacted to and evaluated. For the traits that concern him, the poet defines (demarcates, delineates) an order, an ordinal location. He maps a psychological road by which such an order can be reached. He communicates a *sense* of ontological parity, a sense of the equal reality, though not necessarily the equal importance, of all the complexes he deals with. What Coleridge called "poetic faith," unsatisfactorily equated with "the suspension of disbelief," can be salvaged as the sense of the parity of all complexes as complexes. It is the sense of their in-

tegrity as complexes. Poetic imagination is the power to achieve
the kind of trait structure which arouses in others the spirit of
query immanent in that structure. To this end, the word-structure
is as much the work of imaginative power as the domain of traits
explored. The power is not one of entering into or departing from
"reality" but one of shaping complexes in ways that compel an
assent peculiar to exhibitive query. The orders that the poet
builds are perspectives to be occupied.

To arouse the spirit of query. To compel assent. These two
forces which poetry sets in motion to bear fruit are two forms
of the same power. At first the connection between the two may
seem puzzling. Query may breed assent, but does assent breed
query? Assent in poetry, and in art generally, is appropriation
of the product as relevant to the appropriator. In what way it is
relevant, what specific value it has, need not be determined as
part of the initial response. Far from being self-sufficient and
terminal, artistic assent is the renewal of query. It is the beginning
of articulation. To be responsive to a work of poetry is to bring
it into areas other than those which it first touches. The spirit
of query lies in the urge to make a work relevant in new ways—
relevant to one's situation in life, to one's disciplinary concerns,
and to one's sense of the world at large. Thus in poetic assent we
enter the poetic perspective where it intersects with the one we
occupy, even if at first the entrance is encouraged by a false sense
of linguistic accommodation. Yet we enter not primarily because
there is access and continuity but because the perspective is dis-
criminately liberating and fulfilling. We have accepted the poetic
climate: we have become permeated by a sense of the parity of all
complexes. We accept the contrivance of the poet and extend the
sphere of its influence.

In the climate of ontological parity, poetic endeavor can build
orders of complexes with a freedom belonging to no other form of
query involving language. Herein lies one reason for the unique-
ness of poetic judgment and for the monumental amount of
bad poetry in the world. The freedom instinctively felt by those

for whom poetry is the congenial vehicle of utterance is too often understood by them not as freedom from restrictive conceptions of reality but as freedom from validation. As in the moral and social sphere, freedom is mistakenly regarded as deregulated activity and is confused with the sheer exercise of will. This view of what it means to be free is bedfellow to the view that anything can be accomplished with words provided that the motivation and inspiration of the poet, the conditions "within," are just right. Underestimating the relative determinateness, and hence the recalcitrance, of the materials dealt with (not only words in a social vocabulary but the very complexes of meaning that are discriminated) is made even easier by the obsessive emphasis upon "creativity."

The poetic structuring of an order is a structuring indeed. It entails inclusions and exclusions, and beyond this, a policy of inclusion and exclusion, not moment-to-moment choices dictated by feelings of mastery. There are boundaries to every order, flexible as some of them may be. In every order there are relations of various kinds. The maker finds himself coping with what he has not made, though it may have arisen in the process of making. The assimilative dimension of his life, which presupposes and is presupposed by the manipulative, embraces these conditions of finitude, with which it continually dyes judgment. Methodic judgment, as illustrated by poetry, always functions within this more pervasive process. Any complex with which an individual is involved is perforce manipulated by him in some way. Selectiveness is mandatory for the perpetuation of life, and it does not cease to be mandatory on the level of methodic consciousness. The complex that the poet has discriminated is the order that he has constituted. He is obliged to make this order cohesive, to define it, not of course in formal conceptual terms but by achieving for it a character which he himself can identify. He thereby validates for himself a contrivance forcibly initiated and just as forcibly terminated. The freedom that is his to recognize as real whatever he recognizes at all and whatever he raises up or casts down, neither increases nor lessens the obligations of query.

ii

The patterns of poetic diction and the gravity of the poetic flow are thus indices of deep commitments essential to the art. They are proximate attributes that signify broader underlying attributes like the commitment to the exhibitive mode of linguistic utterance, and like the sense of ontological parity. Whoever shares this sense shares the refusal to see any aspect of the world as negated by or reduced to another. He refuses also to deny the reality of a complex that he loathes, or to affirm the "higher" reality of a complex that he prizes. Underlying attributes, of course, are not to be compared with those constituents of poetry which, despite their lasting and recurring value, actually have been found dispensable in the history of the art. Thus any of the rhetorical tropes is dispensable; it is no more essential to the existence of poetry than rhyme or alliteration. Metonymy and metaphor, for example, are present and even common in non-poetic language, and they can be absent from non-poetic as from poetic language. Their force in a poetic order contributes to the complex of value in that order. But part of the force, the appeal, that they have depends upon the fact that the order *is* a poetic order. The deeper poetic significance of the figurative devices, therefore, apart from their intrinsic charm, is to be explained in terms of their achieving values that presuppose the indispensable attributes of poetic judgment.

We are in position now to define another underlying attribute, one which appears to be directly embodied by the unique economy of language and solemnity of movement recognized as poetic. It is closely related to poetry's sense of ontological parity, but it should be formulated independently. We shall describe it as an emphasis upon the *prevalence* of what is, and consequently as communicating a *sense* of prevalence. By "a sense of" (in the two attributes which involve the phrase) is *here* meant a grasp within keenly focussed awareness. The effect of the grasp may continue indefinitely and fluctuate in intensity. It may be enhanced by articulation. It occurs as a characteristic whole, and is repeatedly identifiable; but it is not simple, not instantaneous, not isolated in consciousness, not analyzed, not unanalyzable, and not unrelated to other complexes.[5]

Think of any natural complex at random—a feeling of hopefulness, a large iceberg. Each of these has an integrity: it is what it is, as distinct from any other complex. But there is more to be said about it than what it is and how it differs. *That* it is, implies a sovereignty. The sovereignty consists in *its* being instead of some other. To this sovereignty belongs another fundamental aspect: the complex is *ineradicable,* no matter how short-lived. Being now, or having been, nothing can erase or undo *that.* The mark is made. The complex prevails. The feeling of hopefulness may be ever so brief. Yet whatever its tenure in the world, however limited its scope, it prevails. As a prevalence it is dominant in regard to what else might have prevailed instead of it, and in regard to any other way in which it might have prevailed; these are *excluded.* It is not less and not more of a prevalence than Mount Everest or the laws of arithmetic or *The Brothers Karamazov* or the brothers Karamazov or the possibility of eliminating economic poverty or the hippopotamus I picture walking a tightrope. Each of these is a prevalence, each is a sovereign complex. Each prevails in an order, an order of complexes to which it belongs; and although the orders have very different traits, all the orders and all the traits prevail in one and the same sense. In the same way, the large iceberg does not prevail in any different sense than a small iceberg. In an everyday sense of the term, the victor "prevails" over the vanquished. But metaphysically, the victor prevails as the victor that he is, and the vanquished prevails as the vanquished that he is. And whatever is, prevails in the way that it does.[6] Each is dominant in so far as it is what it is in the way that it is with the scope that it has. A prevalence excludes—it excludes alternatives to itself.

Let us dwell for a moment on the examples just given (Mount Everest, the laws of arithmetic . . .). Would we wish to say that all of these complexes "exist"? Would we wish to say that among them some are actual but do not exist? That some exist but are not actual? That some are possibilities which are neither actual nor existent? This is not the place to resolve such questions. But no matter what the resolution may be, we can say that all of the complexes prevail. Here perhaps the relation between the concept of prevalence and the concept of ontological parity becomes visible. Whatever has been discriminated, whether found or produced, prevails in some order, in the way that it prevails. In whatever order it is located, it is located—be it God, a leprechaun, or Johnny Appleseed. To say, of what is located in an order of complexes, that it is "unreal," is to make a joke of consistency: we would be admitting that it is, and saying that it is not. We cannot say, of what prevails, that it is unreal. We cannot say, of what is, that it does not prevail in any order. The task of query, of course, is to ascertain, among the discriminanda of men, in what *way* they prevail, in *what* order, in what *kind* of order. In the most generic sense, the task of query in so far as query is to be consummated by invention, is to *define*.

Whatever comes to be a poet's concern emerges with a certain dominance from the process of poetic query. It emerges as a prevalence defined. The poet brings a complex into his sphere of methodic judgment, and in the form of a poem defines for it a sovereignty. That a complex should prevail is the source of poetic wonder. That, generally speaking, what prevails should prevail, that it should be what prevails, is a further source of poetic wonder; but on this general level it can be formulated philosophically as the basal sense of mystery.

The poetic shaping of a complex discriminates the aspect of finality in that complex. It exhibits the complex as a finality. It conveys the sense of prevalence.

> Those ships which left
> Side by side
> The same harbor
> Towards an unknown destination
> Have rowed away from one another.[7]

A prevalence is not always starkly delivered for grasp. The textures of poetic judgment submit to classification no more easily than do its themes. In some poetry the texture is tactically fragmented. The reader reconstitutes for himself the pattern of relatedness which enables him to possess the prevalent complex. In the following poem the complex dealt with is identified by an abruptly suggested kinship of traits, but the depth of the kinship emerges more slowly. The dominant metaphor is at first spread out, as it were in apprehensive pieces, and then animated as if by electric shock.

> Traffic, the lion, the sophisticate,
> facing the primitive, alabaster,
> the new fallen snow
> stains its chastity the new shade
>
> Use defames! the attack disturbs our sleep
>
> This is the color of the road, the color
> of the lion, sand color
>
> —to follow the lion, of use or usage,
> even to church! the bells achime
> above the fallen snow!
>
> —all follow the same road, space.

The pieces wax into a horrific whole, the prevalence of which takes the form of irrevocability.

> Winter, the churned snow, the lion
> flings the woman, taking her
> by the throat upon his gullied

shoulders—shaking the weight fast
and unmolested plunges with her
among the trees—where the whiteness
sparkles—to devour her there:
transit to uses: where the traffic
mounts, a chastity packed with lewdness,
a rule, dormant, against the loosely
fallen snow—the thick muscles
working under the skin, the head
like a tree-stump, gnawing: chastity
to employment, lying down bloodied
to bed together for the last time.[8]

To name a prevalence, apart from the poem's way of naming; to pinpoint it by a phrase, is anticlimactic when plausible, but is implausible most of the time. To speak of what a poem is "about" has always been considered easier in the case of long poems, especially narrative and dramatic poems. But this is the impression that results from dwelling on the story-aspect rather than on the complex of the whole taken in its prevalence. Among the frequent patterns of texture in poetry are a chain of perceptions without emphasis upon continuity, a theme and variations, an expression and determination (or complication) of a paradox, a disputation, a protestation. Accordingly, the sense of prevalence may be conveyed by a grouping of subaltern complexes rather than by the delineation of a single prevalence corresponding to the physical singleness of the poem. Often when the primary subject of poetic query is a complex of feeling, and when the work assumes the role of extracting it from a medley of events and repressions, the emergent prevalence will be least satisfactorily identifiable by a verbal tag. The difficulty may be present no matter what the poetic complex, but especially when the texture is in the form of a conversation, a soliloquy, an aesthetic or moral commentary; when the idiom is admonitory, entreating, or didactic; and when the thrust is a critical observation (accented, in the following poem, by a melancholy humor).

Write as you will
In whatever style you like
Too much blood has run under the bridge
To go on believing
That only one road is right.

In poetry everything is permitted.

With only this condition, of course:
You have to improve on the blank page.[9]

To identify non-poetically the burden of a poetic sense of prev-
alence is a problem similar to that of identifying non-philosophi-
cally the burden of a philosophic emphasis. One cannot presume
to render pithily what the poet and philosopher have rendered
in a structure of configurations and categories. The problem can
be dealt with only in terms of the most delicate articulation. We
have said that the sense of prevalence is not a "simple feeling."
The other side of the coin is that the sense of prevalence does not
always and necessarily fasten itself upon a clearly separate
datum. We should not expect *The Faerie Queene* or the *Iliad* to
provide a grand oneness of poetic discrimination but rather a
world in which there are varieties of awareness and in which the
level of intensity undulates. Poetry in which the physical mag-
nitude of the product is a challenge to assimilation inevitably
contains elements of non-poetic art. It inevitably contains fertile
and arid areas. For the sense of prevalence it can provide the
greatest possible sustenance, but by the most irregular paths.
Long poems are the best preventive of the possible suspicion that
a sense of prevalence must be "intellectual" or coldly spectatorial.
They show that this sense is fundamental, yet not always in the
forefront of attention; pervasive in its presence, yet not competi-
tive with detail.

As if to underscore the difficulty of readily isolating the major
prevalence, the title of the poem from which the following lines
are drawn is part of the poem and not more significant than any
other pair of words that the poem contains. Its function as title,

instead of identifying a central trait, is to lead us into a concat-
enation of sea, land, sky, and value. The rhyme firms the ex-
hibitive structure, and guards against the collapse of the con-
catenation into a miscellany.

THE FISH

wade
through black jade.
    Of the crow-blue mussel-shells, one keeps
    adjusting the ash-heaps;
        opening and shutting itself like

an
injured fan. . . . . .
        The water drives a wedge
    of iron through the iron edge
        of the cliff; whereupon the stars,

pink
rice-grains, ink
    bespattered jelly-fish, crabs like green
    lilies, and submarine
        toadstools, slide each on the other.

All
external
    marks of abuse are present on this
    defiant edifice—
        all the physical features of

ac-
cident—lack
    of cornice, dynamite grooves, burns, and
    hatchet strokes, these things stand
        out on it; the chasm-side is

dead.
Repeated
    evidence has proved that it can live
    on what cannot revive
        its youth. The sea grows old in it.[10]

The generic burden in a poetic work is not: this is what has here been found to be; but rather: this is what has here been found indomitably and unaccountably to be; or: here is a relation of traits sovereign unto itself and irreducible. In the same way that the details of a complex are illuminated by the complex seen as prevailing, the moral aspects of a complex, though in one respect made subordinate by the emphasis on prevalence, in another are sharpened by it: the ships have rowed away from one another. In countless poems a moral complex is itself the prevalence shaped.

It is important not to think of prevalence solely on the model of some familiar complex, just as it is important not to think of what is "real" as basically a space-time existent. Since the real can be an individual or a society of individuals, an actuality or a possibility, a whole or any part of a whole, or any part of a part, an unchanging complex or a changing one—any of these reals can be understood as prevailing. To think of a prevalence is not necessarily to think of what is fixed or unchanging. That is one kind of prevalence. A process as well as a structure, a decline as well as a rise, a recurrence as well as a unique event, a probability as well as an occurrence, prevail in the way that they prevail. All of them can be said to be sovereign, exclusive, ineluctable. Brief or protracted, great or small, a complex in its prevalence excludes what is contrary to its integrity. Here the theoretical and the common conception of prevalence meet. A river, in its process of flow, prevails in so far as it continues to flow. It prevails "against" opposition. Sunshine prevails in so far as it is not beclouded; it prevails against clouds. We can begin to perceive the ordinal conditions of any prevalence. A complex which ceases to prevail in one respect (in one order) may prevail in another. A man who no longer prevails as employer may prevail as employee; a man who ceases to prevail as lover necessarily prevails as acquaintance; so that ceasing to prevail in an order may mean either newly prevailing in another or continuing to prevail in another.

In shaping a complex the prevalence of which is the object of wonder, the poet does not completely determine its constituent traits. Neither does he merely discover these traits and appropriate them. The traits of his invention presuppose traits out of which they are invented. Methodic judgment, in so far as it yields judgments, entails appropriation of a complex which will provide the materials for another. Complexes are selected, but selected from a more pervasive complex. In all poetic judgment there is both an encountering and a re-ordering of complexes. We cannot structure in a given way what lacks the capacity to be structured in that way. On the other hand, what we encounter is encountered because we were seeking. It is eligible as material because it conforms to aims. Thus the prevalence to which a poem directs us by its attributes of diction, sound, and pace cannot be either merely discovered or wrought with complete arbitrariness. Poetic discrimination informs the entire process of contrivance. The poet discriminates traits whether he is concerned with death on the road or with the plight of Psyche. And the product contrived, be it compounded out of the exceeding strange or the strangely familiar, exhibits a sovereign complex. When we find ourselves

> Where Alph, the sacred river, ran
> Through caverns measureless to man
> Down to a sunless sea

we are not disoriented. The hauntingly remote presupposes the known and available. Rivers and caverns, the complexes shaped, are also the complexes found.

The kind of exhibitive judgment that can be called poetic, then, is the product of query that defines a complex as prevalent, thereby contriving to convey a sense of the complex as ineluctably what it is. It should be needless to say that conveying a sense is not opposed to promoting understanding. We have seen that, once conveyed, it is the beginning of responsive query, or articulation.

A significant avenue toward discernment of the poetic sense of prevalence is the kind of poetry which shapes its complex with a certain extreme of ruthlessness. For we may be inclined to think of the sense of prevalence in terms of celebrating what is. Thus W. H. Auden says that poetry responds to "sacred" beings and sacred presences. "The sacred is that to which it is obliged to respond." Moreover, a sacred being "cannot be anticipated; it must be encountered." It "may be attractive or repulsive . . . but this condition is absolute, that it arouse awe." And "all poetry . . . must praise all it can for being and for happening." [11] Now the poetic sense of prevalence may or may not embrace the presence of "sacred" beings. It is a sense which may or may not involve awe. It may or may not be disposed to praise. But the wonder that it involves admits of a far more detached awareness, and reflects a process of invention utterly unruled by reverential or numenal consciousness. It may be "obliged to respond"— where it is accurate to speak of the poet himself as responding— but not necessarily in a spirit of glad union. The four succeeding pieces of poetry, here characterized as works of ruthless exhibitive judgment, happen to be marked by a strain of bitterness, and by a perception of incommensurables that prevail in the human situation.

> Like a skein of loose silk blown against a wall
> She walks by the railing of a path in Kensington Gardens,
> And she is dying piece-meal of a sort of emotional anaemia.
>
> And round about there is a rabble
> Of the filthy, sturdy, unkillable infants of the very poor.
> They shall inherit the earth.
>
> In her is the end of breeding.
> Her boredom is exquisite and excessive.
> She would like some one to speak with her,
> And is almost afraid that I will commit that indiscretion.[12]

It is possible for the coolness of such a delineation to be present even when the complex delineated harbors passions of the most deep-seated kind. Observe, now, passions side by side, vibrating but not in process. Neither is before or after the other, though a past and a future are locked in the compresence that prevails.

By the rivers of Babylon, there we sat down, yea, we wept, when we remembered Zion.

We hanged our harps upon the willows in the midst thereof.

For there they that carried us away captive required of us a song; and they that wasted us required of us mirth, saying, Sing us one of the songs of Zion.

How shall we sing the Lord's song in a strange land?

If I forget thee, O Jerusalem, let my right hand forget her cunning.

If I do not remember thee, let my tongue cleave to the roof of my mouth; if I prefer not Jerusalem above my chief joy.

Remember, O Lord, the children of Edom in the day of Jerusalem; who said, Rase it, rase it, even to the foundation thereof.

O daughter of Babylon, who art to be destroyed; happy shall he be, that rewardeth thee as thou hast served us.

Happy shall he be, that taketh and dasheth thy little ones against the stones.[13]

In the poetry of ruthless discrimination, irony is not a necessary constituent. But it can enter aptly when the prevalence of a complex is seen in the form of irreversibility.

> Since thou hast view'd some Gorgon, and art grown
>   A solid stone:
> To bring again to softness thy hard heart
>   Is past my art.
> Ice may relent to water in a thaw;
> But stone made flesh Loves Chymistry ne're saw.
>
> Therefore by thinking on thy hardness, I
>   Will petrify;
> And so within our double Quarryes Wombe,
> Dig our Loves Tombe.
> Thus strangely will our difference agree;
> And, with our selves, amaze the world, to see
> How both Revenge and Sympathy consent
> To make two Rocks each others Monument.[14]

When a condition in the universe is overwhelming in its hellish-
ness, such as Decay, there are at least three ways of meeting it:
emotional frenzy, retreat, or dissection of the condition. The last
of these, in the form of poetic control, is the demarcation of a
prevalence.

> Remember now, my Love, what piteous thing
>   We saw on a summer's gracious day:
> By the roadway a hideous carrion, quivering
>   On a clean bed of pebbly clay,
>
> With legs flexed in the air like a courtesan,
>   Burning and sweating venomously,
> Calmly disclosed its belly, ironic and wan,
>   Clamorous with foul ecstasy.
>   .   .   .
> The flies swarmed on that putrid vulva; then
>   A black tumbling rout would seethe
> Of maggots, thick like a torrent in a glen,
>   Over those rags that lived and seemed to breathe.
>   .   .   .
> —And even you will come to this foul shame,
>   This ultimate infection,
> Star of my eyes, my being's inner flame,
>   My angel and my passion!
>
> Yes: such shall you be, O queen of heavenly grace,
>   Beyond the last sacrament,
> When through your bones the flowers and sucking grass
>   Weave their rank cerement.
>
> Speak, then, my Beauty, to this dire putrescence,
>   To the worm that shall kiss your proud estate,
> That I have kept the divine form and the essence
>   Of my festered loves inviolate.[15]

iii

We have been saying that the movement of poetic language, its
incisiveness and solemnity, and the way we are impelled to actu-

alize its sound derive from the need to convey a basic and otherwise unrendered dimension of what is, the dimension of prevalence. These features of poetic language are the recognition of prevalence communicating itself, but they are also the means whereby it does so. It could be said that in order to convey the sense of prevalence there has been wrought and spoken the kind of language that is the language of poetry. Poetry cannot be venerated provincially as the attempt to convey in language "what there is"; all disciplines of literature, science, and philosophy one way or another convey in language what there is. The poetic judgment of complexes as prevalent goes hand in hand with the commitment of poetry to judge all complexes as real regardless of the sort of complexes they are, and with the commitment to judge them exhibitively.

Poetry's recognition of the prevalent is indeed a recognition. Science, after all—and any discipline of query—communicates what it has found to prevail. The radical difference between poetry and other disciplines (at least other disciplines communicating in language), with respect to the prevalences they find, lies in the nature of the communicative burden. What poetry judges to prevail it communicates *as* prevailing, *as* sovereign and ineluctable. This is what is implied by saying that poetry conveys the *sense* of prevalence. Each poetic work conveys the sense of *a* prevalence (or of different prevalenc*es*). And a *generalized* sense of prevalence also may supervene to deepen the grasp of prevalences, as may a generalized sense of parity where complexes have become habitually accepted for what they are.

The centrality of the sense of prevalence in no way subordinates the value of the poetic product's constituents or of its exhibitive devices and techniques. On the contrary, the basis or ground of poetic wonder cannot shade the importance of the means which build that wonder. The phases of poetic discrimination, which include the linguistic and rhythmic ingenuities essential to the shaping of its complexes, even may have a value in dissociation from the total product. There is value in the constituents as well as in what they constitute, and in parts judiciously separated from the whole. The main point is that the specific characteristics of the poetic complex are ultimately what convey the sense of prevalence. Yet we must not tilt the scale too far in the other direction, either. It is true that sound, pace, and signification in language are powerful enough to yield pleasurable effect and even to stimulate query apart from poetry, and no matter what the mode of judgment may be. But to be able to speak of sound and signification as poetic sound and signification; of mood, language, and stance as poetic; of the details of a complex dealt with as having not any kind of value but specifically poetic value; of pleasurable effect as poetically pleasurable effect; of a felicitous discrimination as a poetically felicitous discrimination, we need to recognize an implicit confluence of all the elements into a prevalence, into the ineluctable being of the complex before us.

How shall we account for the presence of a poetic strain in a linguistic work that is not a poem and even in a work not intended as an instance of literary art? Mill cautions, no doubt wisely, against regarding as poetry what might often be better described as eloquence. There is a strong inclination to call poetic any segment of a prose work which moves us through its depth of feeling. And yet it would seem that certain forms of eloquence deserve to be regarded as poetic. It would seem also that there are aspects of prose which not only should be regarded as poetic but for which the term "eloquent" is unsatisfactory. We may proceed by considering three questions: (1) Within literary art, what is the essential difference between a narrative poem and the kind of narrative commonly called a novel? (2) What is the difference between two novels, one of which is said to have and the other not to have a poetic aspect? (3) What constitutes a poetic aspect of works belonging to disciplines of query not primarily intended as literary art?

(1) The narrative poem and the narrative novel are both works of exhibitive judgment. (It seems that we must accept the exist-

ence of "non-narrative" novels.) Neither is primarily an attempt to substantiate truth-claims. Neither admits of exemplification by a product which can be meaningfully said to replace, supersede, or render invalid another product. But the novel to a greater extent than the poem tends to preserve the form of assertive language, its word-structures being for the most part declarative, at least to the extent that they carry the weight of the narrative and define the temporal order (not necessarily the successiveness) of its events. The exhibitive aspect of the narrative poem is more evident from the freedom to ignore syntactical conventions and from the utilization of a visible linguistic scheme that announces a unique type of emphasis.

Each of the two narratives may proceed by portraying the history of an individual, into which other individuals, events, and social forces enter; or each may plunge us into a community of individuals, so that the community rather than the individual history is the encompassing order; or each may produce an order wherein conflicting values receive the major share of attention; or each may structure its space and time as the encompassing order. The difference between them lies in the nature of the exhibitive emphasis. The emphasis of the novel is on the history *as* a history, on the characters *as* characters, on the conflicts and values *as* conflicts and values. The emphasis of the poem is on the history, the characters, the conflicts and values, as prevalences. Within the poem, what emerges in prime relief may be an overarching prevalence, such a prevalence in relation to subaltern prevalences, or a plurality of prevalences with an indeterminate bond. Persons, places, and values are as important to the narrative poet as they are to the novelist—but not in the same artistic light, not in the same direction of query. From this contrast it is clear why we cannot say that poetry is concerned with whatever is in so far as it is. For what is can "be" specifically as a history, as a character, as a conflict, as a value; or it can "be" specifically as a prevalence. The "as" in the first sense is the focus of the novel; the "as" in the second sense is the focus of poetry.

(2) The presence of a poetic strain in a novel is not explainable
on the basis of the contrast just made. That is to say, if a novel is
to have a poetic dimension it will not be because the novel ap-
proximates to the character of a narrative poem. The novel's own
narrative character has to be modified. And yet again, to think
of a poetic aspect as present in virtue of the modification is very
different from identifying it with some particular effect. A novel
does not acquire a poetic dimension by inserting a poem into
the narrative. Joyce's *Ulysses* has a poetic dimension that Field-
ing's *Tom Jones* does not have. This does not mean that Joyce's
structural innovations in the narrative genre by themselves ac-
count for the difference. It means that at best the innovations
are instrumental to the sense of prevalence by which *Ulysses* is
informed. The sense of prevalence cannot be identified with any
one technique or device, even in poems, and cannot be assumed
to be producible in any one manner. It is pervasive, for example,
in Proust, who innovates technically in ways very different from
those of Joyce.

(3) If a poetic strain is more likely to be found in the non-
poetic areas of literary art than in areas of inquiry, perhaps the
reason is that in the former the exhibitive mode of judgment is
already present. In philosophy and in religious reflection the
circumstances of a poetic strain are more obscure. An exhibitive
dimension may be present, but why exhibitive judgment there
should take on a poetic character seems to call for explanation.
Obviously it will not do to infer the actual presence of a poetic
component by finding typical conditions under which this compo-
nent might be expected. Given exhibitive linguistic judgment, our
criterion of the poetic strain is the probing of a complex which
issues in the sense of prevalence. Yet why should this be found
where it is found? The answer must be clear cut: the very same
turn of the interrogative temper that directs the poet habitually,
directs the philosopher or religious inquirer on occasion. It is
reasonable to think of philosophic or religious query as informed,
now by the kind of wonder that seeks to be appeased, now by the

kind of wonder that perpetuates itself. Why an exhibitive mani-
festation of the sense of prevalence comes when it does in the
midst of non-poetic judgment, is in part a problem of biography
or empirical psychology. But in greater part it is the outcome of
a profound need by the practitioners of certain disciplines to
occupy a different perspective of judgment within the process of
query. Where a judgment in this perspective causes us to wonder
at a given complex that obtains in the world, we may be able
to differentiate poetry from eloquence. In any such judgment the
power of discrimination coincides with the power of contrivance.
Thus where religious reflection expressed in language merges
with the temper of art, the conditions are ripe for poetry. It is
not surprising to encounter and acquire the sense of prevalence
more frequently in the work of the prophet than in the work of
the philosopher. The one is given to dealing with his relevant
complexes *as* prevailing; the other, with *what* complexes prevail.
St. Paul and St. Augustine basically face in the same direction.
But in Paul the poetic predominates over the theoretical and the
argumentative; in Augustine it is the other way.

In ascertaining whether a poetic strain is present in an other-
wise non-poetic context, can we also preserve emphasis upon
the presence of the sense of ontological parity? Or must we limit
the latter to the order of deliberate poetic invention, to the dis-
cipline of poetry as contrasted with non-methodic manifestations
of the poetic temper? Can it be present implicitly, regardless of
an intellectual repudiation of it? A prime difficulty here is that
Plato, the most poetic of the major philosophers, is commonly
regarded as a bulwark of the principle of ontological priority.
Forms or Essences, we seem to find him saying, are true Being,
while particulars of any kind are ephemeral, insubstantial shad-
ows. Whether or not this is a satisfactory version of what emerges
from Plato's enormously complicated process of query, it remains
the historical testimony of "Platonism," and it has had great
influence on the metaphysical orientation whereby everything is
fitted somewhere into a scheme of reality-appearance or a hier-

archy of being. But when this is said, what after all is the problem
of the poetic strain in Plato? Take the case not of one who, like
Plato, is known primarily as a philosopher, but of one who is
known primarily as a poet. Is there ever actually a problem of
reconciling his art with the doctrinal commitments that are his
in an extra-poetic perspective? We study and note the relations
among the perspectives that he occupies, but we do not find it
impossible that he should assume different postures. The poet's
belief-structure may provide him with material for poetic judg-
ment, as may his economic experience and his emotional prob-
lems. But his exhibitive query is no more subject to an accounting
in terms of assertive judgment than the figures of Jesus and Mary
dealt with by painters are subject to an accounting in terms of
the theological doubts that these painters hold. In the case of a
philosopher, it is customary to expect an effort on his part to
integrate all that appears in his work. That this expectation is
precisely inapplicable to Plato among all others is no accident.
The assertive and the exhibitive aspects of philosophy are not
two ways of "saying" one and the same "thing." They do not
both "say," and as two different modes of judging natural
complexes they are no more "opposed" than are dancing and
carpentry or dreaming and weaving. The relation we are entitled
to expect among constituent aspects of a philosophic outlook is
that of mutual enhancement and complementation, not that of
formal consistency. For consistency is a norm applicable to what
is produced in the assertive aspect. Perhaps in asking whether
different modes of judgment enhance one another within a larger
structure, we mean to ask whether the presence of each in that
structure sharpens awareness of the integrity and value of the
other.

Commitment to ontological parity in the poetic art is non-
domination by appearance-reality schemes or hierarchies of
being. It is not a "postulate" of poetry, not a concept necessarily
present to the poet's consciousness. It is a name for his freedom
to explore exhibitively what there is to explore. In no philosopher

is the scope of exhibitive judgment so great as it is in Plato. In this area of his query the poetic strain is recurrent and deep. The prevalence he most impressively conveys is that of *query itself*. The dialogue form is inherently exhibitive and (in Plato) militantly non-categorical. Within it is to be found the intricate pattern of myth and theoretic analysis which, in its total impact, reinforces the predominantly exhibitive character of Plato's method. If, then, there is a doctrine of ontological priority in Plato, it must be considered a result of theoretic probing that does not exhaust the multifariousness of his outlook and does not restrict him as poet. The poetic Plato finds before him an inexhaustible array of complexes all equally deserving of query.

VII

KNOWLEDGE, ACTUALITY, AND ANALYSIS IN POETRY

i

When we see that poetry is judicative though it does not function assertively, we also can see that it is capable of achieving knowledge by means of exhibitive query. The conception of knowledge as solely propositional stands opposed to an acceptance not of poetic knowledge alone but of artistic knowledge generally. If poetry in order to be cognitive must contain true propositions, then presumably some of its cognitive efforts are unsuccessful and must be represented by false propositions that it puts forth. We have had occasion to see that such a treatment of poetry as pseudo-science reflects the further confusion of equating the whole of query with inquiry.

Under the influence of pragmatist philosophers a connection of one kind or another has often been made between meaning and action (experimental or personal action), and between knowledge and action. More recently knowledge has been admitted by certain philosophers to take the form of "knowledge how" as well as "knowledge that" or "knowledge about" or "knowledge of." What the various pragmatists and other philosophers have not seen is that action itself is a mode of judgment rather than a means of bringing us beyond judgment to make it intelligible, valid, or effective. Nor have they seen that knowledge as non-propositional must be judicative nevertheless.

In order for the notion of exhibitive knowledge to be persuasive, we must at least point the way toward a more adequate view of knowledge in general. A more adequate view, by recognizing art as cognitive, would not denigrate science, and by recognizing poetry in particular as cognitive, would not push it to the top of a cognitive hierarchy, in the compensative manner of apologetic art theory. Indeed, the resultant conception would be of the kind that recognizes different types of knowledge, dependent upon different orders of common life and different orders of query, and does not recognize a single, non-ordinal, absolute hierarchy. So that, as we once stated the matter, "Physics, history, and poetry are cognitive in different respects, not in different degrees."

We have seen that poetry, in so far as it communicates to willing respondents, inculcates an impetus to query, of whatever mode, stimulating articulation or utilization of the poetic product. This is only a stricter way of formulating the idea that poetry communicates effectively when it perpetuates the temper of the poetic process. But it is also a more accurate way, because continuing query inspired by poetry may not itself be poetic in the sense of producing poetry. The poetic process should be construed to embrace all that is pertinent to poetic production and its articulation. Now poetic knowing is one aspect of what happens as the poetic process is pursued or articulated. Typically, we speak sometimes of "knowing" and sometimes of "knowledge." To get to know is to make a certain kind of gain. To know, to have knowledge, is to have acquired a certain kind of power. For the gain made is not a gain if it cannot be exemplified on more than one occasion. Knowing is not a unique or unrepeatable event, but rather the recurrent actualization, in various forms, of a possibility. In knowing, we must be able to make a comparison with, construct in an envisaged way, or act in a tried way toward, a given complex. This is not all: To be cognitive, a specific power of judging, along with its actualizations, must be one that is required for the augmentation of the order in which it functions. The actualizations must be depended upon. They must be needed and not be gratuitous. They must have a compulsive character. We cannot decide to know what we know. The decision we make in this regard lies in the seeking of knowledge. The compulsiveness is the validity or "objectivity" or efficacy that belongs to knowledge.

Poetic knowledge is "knowledge through"—knowledge through contrivance, or through the articulative expansion of contrivance. The knowledge peculiar to poetry is a gain made, by poet and respondent, in virtue of exhibitive query, and carried forward from one project to another or from one phase of a project to another. The gain is "measured," like certain other types of cognitive gain, by the extent of its applicability either in the order of poetic invention or the order wherein poetry is articulated. If the gain is a power to discern a certain type of trait, and has therefore enhanced actual discernment, it can be reactualized in the continuation of query. We cannot demand to be told "what" it is that has been gained in poetry, and "how" it will be applied, if what we are demanding is propositional specification. But we can demand articulation of the cognitive process in poetry. Critically, we can show how specific themes and stratagems bear cognitive relevance to other themes and stratagems, in a particular poem, a particular sequence of poems, or a life's work. What the poet knows, he has gained from his discriminations and transmitted in the furtherance of query. What he knows is what he comes to know in the practice of poetry, what he has the power to re-apply and does. It may be applied cumulatively, in a single direction. Or it may be applied not cumulatively but for the purpose of reversing an earlier disposition, varying a discriminative trend. What he has come to know in either case, however, is what compels him to work (judge) in the way that he does. The absence of knowledge from the poetic process would mean utter discontinuity, non-relatedness among the instances of methodic activity. Once again, if we are addicted to asking questions about degree of evidence or certainty we are re-introducing a conception of knowledge pertinent to the assertive mode of judgment. We can say that the poet's knowledge may not be applied by him in a way that turns out to be poetically best—however required it may be for *his* poetry. Knowledge is only one aspect of poetic query. What may be more important for the poet than applying a specific vein of knowledge is deviation from what he knows, that is, movement by him in a direction less dependent on what he has gained thus far. The poet's cognitive power itself may be feeble. But the validity of such knowledge as he has lies in its being required by him under the conditions of exhibitive judgment.

Generally speaking, we get to know (or gain cognitively), in the sense of acquiring and exercising a power, when we have defined (discriminated) a complex of judgment—active, exhibitive, or assertive—that is different in some respect from any we have hitherto defined, and when we are compelled to utilize this judgment to augment the process of judging in a given order. From this it would follow, strictly, that everyone has knowledge of some kind in some orders of concern, however restricted these orders may be, however insulated from orders of common concern, however remote from what is socially or morally valuable. Every gain in knowledge is to some extent a loss in subsequent freedom of choice, but the elimination of untenable choices ultimately enhances freedom of judgment. The loss is of the kind that makes possible further cognitive gain; and in this way the process of knowing continues. Each restriction is an augmentation. A scientific discrimination and a poetic discrimination alike acquire cognitive value in relation to other discriminations before and after. They augment an order, though in so doing they spoliate some of the possibilities present in the order. As discriminations they cannot be undone. But they can take on changing importance as they are included in further, and on occasion more comprehensive, discriminations. Some knowledge is unmethodical and

even casual or accidental. It may have nothing whatever to do
with query. Cognitive gain may or may not be moral gain. There
is a great deal of knowledge that has made men unhappy and that
makes human woe possible. A major problem of man is the co-
ordination and harmonization of judgments that arise in the
different modes. The spirit of query, aiming at invention in any
mode of judgment, is vulnerable amidst the wider orders within
which the conditions of its continuation are to be found but
which are indifferent, often inimical, to its being.

ii

Although it is the source of humane constructiveness, query has
its rebellious side. It struggles against the forces which sustain
inflexibility of judgment. Poetic query is rebellious in its own
way. To be sure, constancy and continuity are essential to all
methodic judgment, providing for it stable ordinal location and
allowing new promising judgment to germinate. Poetry mingles
linguistic constancy with linguistic invention. But it is the enemy
of standardized language, the language of "correctness." It is
the enemy of narrowness in the conception of clarity, intelligi-
bility, and effective communication. It is the enemy of "indescrib-
ability" and "indefinability," of preconceived "limits of language."
It recognizes no wisdom of language. It is the enemy of "proper
usage," proper syntax, linguistic propriety as such. These militant
attitudes designed to safeguard the inventive possibilities of its
language do not prevent it from being able to respect its own
need for care in moulding detail, from being methodically scru-
pulous, or from being able to accept tradition and the poetic heri-
tage.

What T. S. Eliot approvingly calls "the repeated reminder of
Mr. Pound that poetry should be as well written as prose" [1]
makes no sense at all. Is poetry in so far as it is "well" written
distinguishable from poetry in so far as it is poetry? In what way
is well-writtenness conceived as a norm? Is it a property that

could be exemplified by all poems in the same way? It clearly cannot be a guide to literary activity, for it constitutes no independent ideal but is itself given meaning, and meaning anew, by each product of literature. The injunction to "write well" presupposes conformity to a literary standard preceding each instance of literary endeavor. Such a standard is widely accepted for prose, but primarily (one hopes) because conformity to it is preferable to irresponsible work. The injunction treats the writing of poetry as if each product were a technical exercise. It seems to reflect a literary model which is the one its advocates happen to favor. It seems, moreover, to think of this model as applicable perpetually and without qualification. To urge that poetry be "well written" actually is as vacuous as to urge that poetry be "good" (or that science be "true"). Writing "well" is not prescribed but discovered on the basis of writing that takes place. The writing is what provides the means to determine the "well," to ascertain its possibilities. Those to whom the critical community has assigned secure status seem most willing to erase the line between literary invention and literary conformity. "Writing well" is not, however, a constant that can be conformed to or deviated from. It can be used as a colloquial accolade, but not as a precept. There is something distinctly comic in being ready to say that a particular poem is an outstanding piece of work but not well written, or that a poem is very well written but of negligible poetic value. No; poetry is subject neither to the lazy rules of good form nor to criteria of the right and the proper, even if they are propounded by major poets. It is subject to governance. But that is the governance of query, and in query there is no one model of governance, nor room for the legislation of style.

iii

Just as it has been held that only poetry deals adequately with actuality, so it has been held that poetry never deals with actuality at all. According to S. K. Langer, poetry always makes a "break with actuality." "There is no trafficking with actualities in poetry." In poetry "everything actual must be transformed by imagination into something purely experiential." Poetic events develop in a "virtual world." Each poet by means of words produces "an illusion." He produces "a pure appearance," a "semblance" of events lived and felt, a "piece of virtual life." And "nothing can be built up unless the very first words" of a poem "effect the break with the reader's actual environment." When the virtual world is built up, its poetic or illusory events "have no core of actuality that allows them to appear under many aspects. They have only such aspects as they are given in the telling." [2]

Now on the basis of our investigations it is false that poetry (the poetic product) deals with actuality alone, and false that poetry alone deals with actuality. It is false that poetry necessarily conveys the sense of actuality better than any other discipline. The sense of prevalence need not, of course, be the sense of a prevalent actuality. And it is false, as we now propose to show, that poetry never deals with actuality; that it abandons the actual and that actualities cannot be what it is about.

But to say that poetry can and does deal with actuality may imply (a) that the actuality with which it deals (in its own way) is always actuality in one and the same sense, the sense with which science and common life (in their ways) are concerned; that actualities, in other words, are "just plain actual," no matter what is involved. Or it may imply (b) that the actuality with which it deals can be but need not be actuality in the familiar sense that is commonly believed to be absolute. Our suggestion is that (a) is false, and that (b) is true.

The truth of (b) would be enough to refute the view that poetry, the poetic work as utterance, never is concerned with actuality. But it is equally important to see that, whatever kinds of actuality may be distinguished, there is no evidence that any is foreign or inimical to poetic query. Certain theorists think of actuality as intrinsically antithetical to imagination, so that one cannot deal imaginatively *with* actualities, say by discriminating other actualities within them, or by discriminating them in other actualities. The assumption seems to be that dealing with actuality harnesses us to it, allows it to dominate us. We must make a flight from actuality, and that flight is "imagination." It is easy to see why advocates of such a view recoil from the idea that imagination is required in science. There are other reasons why it is held that poetry must abandon actuality. Is not the actual world confused and chaotic? Poetry must make us see and feel more clearly, more fully; how, then, can it subject itself to the world that is actually before us? It must purify, providing for us an illusion, a "pure experience." Note that in this usage, the "purely experiential" is antithetical to the "actual." It is entirely non-historical, an essence distinguished within the realm of "pure" consciousness.

Query can concern itself with actualities and understand them as actualities; it does not have to aim at the production of illusions or "pure appearances." Its power of discrimination may take a scientific form, a form of assertive judgment; or it may take a poetic form, a form of exhibitive judgment, entailing, as in every art, a process of contrivance. Imagination, the power of query, may discern *in* an actuality what has not been discerned, and produce, through theory or contrivance, what has not been produced. What imagination transforms (scientifically or poetically) need not be the mode of prevalence (in this case, the actuality) but the order in which a given complex has been found to prevail. Both science and poetry are "dominated" by actuality in the sense that they accept a prior determinateness within the actual. But neither is dominated in the sense that it is not free to modify this determinateness and add determinateness in another respect, free to manipulate the actuality. Both are free to take "flight" from it, by probing its possibilities, or by choosing to attach to it traits wholly arbitrary. Any actuality is discriminable in any number of ways. We cannot tell the poet where to exercise his power of query, or what complexes to manipulate.

But now, what if the poet wishes also to dwell upon complexes other than those which scientists and most people call "actualities"? What if he wishes to concern himself not with the prevalence of wars and mountains on earth, of "dappled things" and death, but with the prevalence of Faust, Phaedra, and the Lorelei? Are these last three complexes departures from actuality? No, only from the kinds of actuality which are accessible and identifiable in terms of certain habitual public standards. Faust, Phaedra, and the Lorelei are products. But Congress, heavenly bodies, and London also are products. They are products of physical nature or society, rather than products of art and legend. All products have their traits of actuality and traits of possibility. The space and time of Faust, his traits of character and conduct, are actual in his world, a poetically produced order. As such they are determinately contrastable both with the traits of others in the same order and with the traits of others in other orders. Faust does not "virtually" make a pact with the devil; he actually does so. The Lorelei does not conceivably sing and lure sailors; she actually does so. It is possible for Phaedra to desire men other than her husband; actually she desires her step-son. Of this actuality there are many witnesses, such as Euripides and Racine, who try to define and interpret its limits. A public, socially produced actuality in common astronomically measured time and an actuality artistically produced cannot, either of them, combine contradictory traits. As we read, we know that Faust will possibly evade a reckoning with the devil and possibly not evade a reckoning. But we know that he cannot actually evade a reckoning and actually not evade it. The Lorelei cannot actually destroy and actually not destroy sailors. The time between Faust bargaining his soul and the devil claiming it is not an illusion; the time is the actual time that it is in the legendary and poetic order. It is not public time in the sense that we as readers can be subject to that temporal order as we live our biological life spans. But the order is accessible to us in various ways. It is intelligible to us in virtue of traits common to both orders. The poet is able to communicate because any order he chooses for poetic query is at some point continuous with the order in which traits identified by standard social procedures prevail.

This conception shows the idea of actuality to be viable only in respect to an order of natural complexes. It is an ordinal conception of actuality. The kind of actuality present in an order depends upon the kind of order that it is. The regnant philosophic conception of actuality assumes a single unqualified "realm" to which every complex that is discriminated belongs if we are to credit it with being actual. On this conception, Marlowe or Goethe is an actuality but Faust is not: the actual is the actual, the fictitious is the fictitious. Such a conception is one form which the principle of ontological priority takes. Instead of speaking unqualifiedly about what is real and what is not, it speaks in an unqualified but comparably reckless way about what is actual and what is not—without regard to the pertinence of the question, actual in what respect? or the question, actual in terms of what conditions and traits? This orthodox view usually relies upon some everyday physical "thing" as its paradigm of actuality. But it cannot account for what makes physical actuality actuality if it recognizes only physical actuality. If it wishes to reason about physical actualities, it must recognize logical actuality, wherein, for example, one proposition actually is implied by the postulates of a logical order while another proposition actually is not. In the same way, if it did not recognize moral, legal, political, economic, or poetic actualities, much that it ordinarily considers to be intelligible would not be intelligible at all.

"But can I grasp the hand of Faust?" No, but you cannot grasp the hand of George Washington, either. The space of Washington's movements is indeed not the same as the space of Faust's, but you can be related to the space of either by interpreting it in terms of your space—in terms of complexes common to all three orders. An inevitable objection to the ordinal view of actuality will take this form: "The so-called actualities in the realm of fiction are seen not to be actualities as soon as we ask whether they can cause things to happen. A true actuality is efficacious. It has effects. A literary character is the effect of its creator. It has no effects of its own." Now this objection can be met handily. It rests on two related confusions. The first has to do with the notion of the efficacious. If this notion is arbitrarily and stubbornly restricted to physical efficacy in public space, then any broader approach to efficacy is ruled out in advance. The wise question to ask, so far as the objection to an ordinal theory of actuality is concerned, is not whether literary creatures are efficacious, but in what sense efficacy can belong to literary creatures. The second confusion has to do with the conditions under which efficacy is to be ascertained. A complex may be considered with regard to its effect on other complexes belonging to the order wherein it is produced and defined. Or it may be considered with regard to its effect on complexes of another order significantly related to its own. For it may prevail as a complex in both orders. To illustrate: we can ask whether the character Faust is efficacious in the poetic order wherein it was produced. We can also ask whether the character Faust is efficacious in the historic order of civilization, or more specially, in the order of criticism and appreciation. That Faust is efficacious in relation to other characters of the poetic order in which he prevails, that he actually affects them, that to him are to be attributed acts and attitudes not attributable to others, can be easily verified. That Faust is efficacious in relation to persons and moral viewpoints belonging to the order of recorded history, can also be easily verified. And it is the efficacy of Faust that we are talking about, not the efficacy of Goethe. In the last analysis, efficacy consists in the difference that a complex makes by being that complex. Every prevalence makes a difference.

Poetry, far from making a break with actuality, cannot possibly do so. Specific poems may ignore specific actualities; that is, any actuality which may have been encountered in various overlapping orders may be excluded from the actualities in a poetic order—though it may also be included. But a poetic order has actualities of its own. And the actualities in the poetic order cannot be meaningful and yet totally unrelated to actualities in other orders of human life.

iv

We have noted (in Chapter III) the allegation that prose does and poetry does not "analyze." To ascribe a function of this kind to prose *as such;* to find it in the work of all who do no more than compose deliberately—every diarist, journalist, philosopher, demagogue, theologian, preacher, novelist—seems incredible, mainly because being analytical so often suggests keenness and precision. We may, however, think of the activity as admitting of better and worse practice. Then the problem is to determine what it means for judgment to have an analytical aspect.

We shall try to clarify the notion of analytical activity as such. In so doing, we must continue to speak, in generic terms, of judgment rather than language; for only in this way do we allow the possibility that analysis may be present in the various arts. Our attention here, of course, is primarily directed to poetry. But it will be desirable to proceed by mediating, as it were, between those disciplines which are most widely acknowledged to have an analytical aspect, namely the sciences, and those which, like the arts, are rarely believed to have it. One way to mediate is to focus initially and carefully on philosophy, which of all disciplines most essentially requires both assertive and exhibitive judgment. Here as before, in order to arrive at an adequate conclusion about the relation between analysis and poetry, our patience may have to be sorely tried. But the nature of analytical activity in philosophy is of equal and intrinsic importance.

The term "analysis" is old, and the kind of activity it represents has been a respectable one since the time of the Greek philosophers and mathematicians. From lexicographic sources we find that the Greek word has a fair number of contexts which contribute to its range of meaning. It can suggest undoing, or regressing. And it can suggest loosening, or dissolving, or reducing, or breaking up a whole into parts, or resolving a problem. Among its antonyms, "analysis" seems to have had two that are related but distinguishable—"genesis" and "synthesis." So that in one of its senses, analysis implied tracing back as contrasted with originating or making or creating; and in another sense, it implied separating as contrasted with putting together. Now we need not abandon the framework implicit in so long-established a usage. But unless this framework is depicted in rather different terms and reformulated with better conceptual tools, it will remain cloudy.

In various disciplines of assertive judgment whose common purpose is inquiry, practitioners seem not only clear about what they consider to be instances of analyzing, but also in basic agreement on why an instance *is* an instance. The question what similarities and differences there are among these various scientific disciplines with respect to the activity each calls "analyzing" is fortunately one that we are not directly concerned with. In any effort to identify the analytical process within a type of query like philosophy, and to formulate some of its features abstractly, the principal danger is provincialism—an unhistorical and often euphoric conviction that the process is solely exemplified, the procedure "really" practised, by such-and-such a movement. That we should be able to agree on some outstanding instances of the activity we are trying to interpret, makes sense. But such instances represent a beginning. It is insufficient to answer a specific need of formulation by saying that if we read the work of this or that person, we will know what it means to analyze. In effect this is what has been done by more than one historian of the most recent analytical movement in philosophy. These historians expound the views of writers whose activity is called "analytical," but do not say what makes their activity, and not that of their contemporaries, analytical. Reading what the representatives of an activity have written may show effectively but does not explain and formulate what they are supposed to be representing in common. Nor can the advice to read and attend be justified as an ostensive technique of clarification. It is too often an appeal to obviousness in an issue that is far from obvious and that would seem to demand the very activity under consideration. But this "ostensive" approach is by no means unusual; it stems from a strong trend to be found primarily within Anglo-American philosophy of the twentieth century. G. E. Moore, in defending his version of common-sensism, was always pained when asked to formulate some identifying characteristics of "common sense." He could only understand such a request as a sign that more examples were required. The same result emerges from the later work of Wittgenstein, who so often urges us to be content with family resemblances and not to hunt vainly and misleadingly for supposed common traits. No sooner are we content in a given case than we find Wittgenstein confounding the formulation of the family resemblances, or the principle of their connection in *that* family, with the introduction of more members of the family.

There are philosophers who seem to believe that any activity rightly called "analysis" necessarily has language as its subject-matter. No doubt we could live with the view that economic analysis, psychoanalysis, artistic analysis, or chemical analysis ought to be re-named. But the view that *as* analyses such activities probe only verbal complexes, can only be regarded as outlandish.

Let us consider first the traditional and persisting notion of analysis as somehow involving wholes and parts, and as stressing an activity that proceeds in one direction, namely, reducing or breaking up wholes into parts. Taken by themselves, metaphors like "breaking up" or "dissolving," which are used to suggest an activity, leave unspecified the rationale of the activity. At the same time, they provoke a type of question which represents in small compass a long-time philosophic issue. Do we want to move from wholes to parts because a part is in some ways more fundamental than a whole? Or do we so move in order the better to understand the whole? What would it mean to say that either is more fundamental than the other? Is there an incommensurateness between an adequate concern with wholeness and an adequate concern with composition? Some descriptions of the movement from whole to part use the expression "reducing a whole to parts"; others, the expression "reducing a whole to *its* parts." Thus an additional set of questions is opened. What does it mean to say that some parts are "proper" parts? Can wholes in any sense be immutable integrities? And if so, how could there be what there surely are and become, wholes which are also parts and parts which are also wholes? When are we justified in speaking of wholes, and when of parts?

There are good reasons why questions directed in these ways, although essential, will not *suffice* to help us clarify the process of analyzing. One is that the notion of "part" is impossibly tricky. If wholes were all like apples, furnaces, boxes, or buildings, the problem might be less refractory. But philosophers have been interested in "wholes" like the state, consciousness, obligation, mathematical system, action, law, poem, perception, the individual. Is intentionality "part" of consciousness? Is a visual image part of consciousness? Are these both parts in the same sense? Is an obligation part of a relation between persons? Is a relation between persons part of an obligation? Are the spaces or pauses between the words of a poem part of the poem? What are the parts of a physical law? Is a rule part of a code? of a system? of a state? Is a traditional procedure part of a system in the sense that a theorem might be said to be part?

The issue arising out of these questions is not whether they can be answered. With suitable qualifications and the enumeration of different senses for "part," they can be made to be answered. We should not, for example, think of all parts as spatially enclosed in that of which they are parts, or as stuck to it in a cluster. The more fundamental issue is whether, by the time we got through qualifying, we could not just as well say that analyzing is the interpreting of parts in terms of wholes, as that analyzing is the interpreting of wholes in terms of parts.

For our purpose it is desirable to discard the whole–part model, if only because of its ambiguities. It seems to be this model, incidentally, which makes people think of analysis as intrinsically praiseworthy, as better or more admirable than other intellectual procedures. Most parents would prefer their children to take apart a machine rather than to contemplate its shape. Most journalists prefer to be news analysts rather than news reporters. Literary critics want to be regarded as analytical. The layman admires those who penetrate to the "inner parts" of things, to the guts; those who peer hard, somewhat along surgical lines, dissecting and cutting, cutting out the bad and sewing up the good. Among philosophers, the notion of analysis has been uncritically taken for granted. It has been found much less controversial than the notions, say, of theory, imagination, or observation. Traditional philosophic critics of analysis, Bergson, for example, have relied no less heavily on the whole–part model for their *negative* conclusions—although it should be pointed out that it is not analysis as such that Bergson denigrates but rather the particular position it is made to occupy in the approach to a subject-matter. Bergson's essential point, methodologically speaking, is that the initial and fundamental stage in the understanding of a subject-matter requires this subject-matter to be seen as a whole without parts.

It is incomparably more useful to think in terms of complexes and traits than in terms of wholes and parts. There are qualitative traits, relational traits, linguistic traits, logical traits; traits are discriminated in various ways; complexes are also traits, and traits also complexes. Such a theoretical shift, which at once makes possible a more flexible approach to the nature of analysis, does not at once free us from pitfalls. To many whose metaphysics reaches no farther than the intuitions that emanate from common usage, "complexes" immediately implies "simples," and therewith the whole–part model is re-introduced. Many also think that analysis cannot be anything but a search for simples, the simples that compose all there is. Aside from this happy faith in simples, they confuse positive doctrines with procedures. For example, they cite the exponents of "logical atomism" as analysts *par excellence*. But a doctrine of atomic facts and atomic propositions has nothing necessarily to do with the *process* of analyzing. If Russell and the early Wittgenstein were analysts in the procedural sense, it was not because they espoused a doctrine of atomic structures with component simples. Doctrines of this general type have been espoused by philosophers using the most diverse procedures, many of them remote from reductive analysis.

Could it be said that at bottom philosophical analyzing is the making of distinctions? Distinctions are to be found on all levels of query, though sometimes antecedent to or in conjunction with query rather than emergent from it. The making of distinctions is one way of discriminating traits. We should not want to *count* the number of distinctions made if we wished to assess analytical power. In principle, distinctions can be multiplied endlessly; in practice, it is the ways in which they are made, the ways in which they are utilized, the purposes which they subserve that are important. Any instance of distinction-making, however rewarding in itself, presumably has a purpose the character of which is not reducible to distinction-making. A set of distinctions is a means, let us say, to the completion of a specific project which provoked and guided the distinctions in the first place and prevented them from being random exercises. In the light of this complication, we might wish to say that in philosophy distinction-making is an indispensable but not a sufficient condition of analyzing. But there are other complications. Multiplying distinctions sometimes may actually interfere with the grading of distinctions. This means that in the practice of analyzing we have to discriminate forms of discrimination as well as traits in the more customary sense. From the standpoint of both common and historical experience, we should not always see fit to represent the analytical temper by the most obvious kind of distinction-making. Thus the analytical temper of Aristotle is not more typically represented by his distinguishing eight senses of the word "in" than by his inquiry into friendship. Nor is the analytical temper of Locke more appropriately exemplified by his distinguishing five senses of the word "but" than by his inquiry into freedom of choice. It would be strange to believe that the inquiry into space and the inquiry into language, in *behalf* of which these distinctions of "in" and "but" are respectively drawn, fall *outside* the province of analytical activity. Would we want to say that analytical activity in these writers begins where a certain paragraph begins?

Sometimes analyzing is conceived not in terms of the number of distinctions made, but in terms of the detail and minuteness of the distinctions. In either interpretation, there is at least tacitly presupposed some standard of measurement by which the analyst can ascertain the progress of a specific analysis. The very mention of minuteness and detail suggests a kind of microscopic analogy, a scrutiny of the smaller than small, making analytical progress to consist in the discernment of ever finer textures. If this does not tend covertly to revive the whole–part model of analysis, it does encourage an assumption that detailed analysis requires appropriately limited subject-matter. Of course, all subject-matter has to be limited in one way or another; it is the principle of limitation that is always in some respect debatable. To suppose that the degree of detail in analysis varies directly with the narrowing of the subject-matter seems ridiculous. Would we want to think of Hume's study of causation, for example, as a narrowing of subject-matter? In such an analysis the forest is not lost to the trees, and there are trees aplenty.

Let us suppose that the complex to be analyzed is not a word, not a concept, not a structure or a process, but rather what we typically call a problem. We want to analyze the kind of prob-

lem it is and the methods and avenues that make its solution pos-
sible. At once the microscopic analogy runs into trouble, for at
the outset there is no obvious area in which we are to peer. We
therefore want to look for whatever is relevant to the diagnosis
and definition of the problem. In this type of search we may have
to range far and wide, and not squint more and more narrowly.
We may, for example, find that another problem offers better
access to the one at hand. We may have to introduce concepts
not originally suspected to be relevant, and we may have to make
other analyses in order to further the ongoing one. And yet it *is*
ongoing. We are still analyzing, and promoting our analysis.
Thus our analysis may entail considerable ramification. It may
not at all fit the conception of a magnifying-glass process. Of
course, we can try to convince ourselves that we are *not* con-
cerned with ramifications and connections, that these represent
other problems. And yet, again, by accepting and dealing with
the ramifications, we may indeed be able to show that we are
progressing in the analytical effort originally undertaken. Some
people would no doubt persist in describing the search for rele-
vant complexes as at best a non-analytical function which *aug-
ments* the analysis. But there has to be a pretty thin line between
what augments an analysis and what enters into that analysis.
What an analysis essentially needs, in order to function as such,
can hardly be deemed extrinsic to it.

The main point is the weakness of the microscopic conception.
And this weakness can be shown in familiar cases. For example,
if we are trying to analyze what an event is (or, what meaning
or meanings belong to the concept of event), we may find that
we cannot separate it from the concept of occurrence. And then
we may find that we need to ask whether there is a difference
between occurrence and becoming. At this stage the subject of
our analysis, and accordingly the analysis, has shown itself to
be not narrowed down or reduced in scope but extended and
more complicated. We may find that event is one aspect of oc-
currence, but we may find instead that occurrence is one aspect

of event. In other words, our analysis may consist in providing a more comprehensive account, the kind of account needed if we are to clarify the concept under examination.

There is a widespread conviction that, whatever analyzing may entail, it is the means of achieving "thoroughness." There is no doubt that "thoroughness" is most often a term of commendation in every discipline that involves inquiry. Nor is there much doubt that practically its instances can be identified without trouble. Clarifying it is another matter. Thoroughness is attributable to a product or activity under certain kinds of circumstances, specifically when this product or activity belongs to a class of roughly similar efforts, efforts that bear direct comparison with the given one. Thus we would say that Mill's *On Liberty* is a thorough piece of work. But we would not say this of Plato's *Symposium*—nor would we say the *opposite*. The *Symposium* is beyond thoroughness and lack of thoroughness. This does not make it sacrosanct, or exempt it in the slightest degree from critical investigation. For certain types of product there does not obtain the problem whether a particular level of virtue is present. Yet both Mill's essay and Plato's dialogue are works of analysis, though not of analysis alone, and indeed of conceptual analysis in an enduring sense of the term, though not of conceptual analysis alone. Naturally enough, we tend to confuse the presence or absence an analysis with the presence or absence of the conventions that identify it for us. But some complexes are analyzed by a kind of frontal attack, others by manipulation of verbal usages, still others (as in Plato) by being rotated, so to speak, delineated successively in a number of perspectives. This last form of analysis, as we shall shortly suggest, is fundamental in the arts.

Where the notion of thoroughness *is* applicable, can we set down any conditions of its attainment, beyond the appeal to obviousness? Probably it is justifiable to say that no matter how far an analysis has gone, no matter how effectively it has dealt with a complex, it can go farther. In matters philosophical, even where the objective is specified and the principle of limitation enunciated, it is dubious to suppose and impossible to demonstrate that all relevant possibilities have been exhausted. In situations of common life we may so shape the requirements of an analysis, and so frame the problem at hand, that we can determine the limits of relevance. This, of course, can be done to some extent in philosophy. In philosophy thoroughness cannot mean completeness. Attributions of thoroughness will vary with the status which certain types of problems and subject-matters occupy in a philosophic community. These attributions will as often depend upon the expectations of philosophers as upon abstract comparison. It is within a community of query that standards of comparison obtain. But of course a community need not take the form of a group of persons deliberately functioning together at a particular period of time.

There is another side to the question of thoroughness. Consider two analyses which have been worked out independently of one another but which seem to draw roughly similar distinctions—for example, Frege's distinction between sense and reference, and Peirce's distinction between interpretant and object. Let us assume, however, that one of these otherwise parallel distinctions applies only to linguistic signs, and that the other applies both to linguistic and non-linguistic signs. The two distinctions are alike based on extensive consideration of practice and use; but one of them, being developed in a more comprehensive framework, has wider theoretical significance than the other. Is one a more thorough analysis than the other? If it is—and it is not implausible to believe that it is—then we would have to draw either of two conclusions: (*a*) the more far-reaching theoretical character of the one inquiry reveals thoroughness in some cases to depend not on the analytical phase but on a non-analytical phase of the inquiry; or (*b*) the far-reaching theoretical awareness is indigenous to one *kind* of analysis. These conclusions indicate, respectively, either that analyzing can only be one among various philosophic functions, or that analyzing can admit of much wider and more inclusive manifestations than the procedure of many philosophers allows. In practice, it is of lesser importance to ask whether a complex has been analyzed, and of greater importance to ask in what way, to what end, and on what level it has been analyzed.

We are ready to formulate, in generic terms, the function and process of analysis, eliminating the primacy of the whole–part approach, avoiding the microscopic conception, and encompassing the sense in which poetry may be said to be analytical.

Analysis is the process whereby a given natural complex is explored with respect to its integrity as a complex rather than with respect to its possible bearing upon the integrity of another complex. It is the emphasis upon the exploration of a complex in so far as other complexes are relevant to it rather than in so far as it is relevant to other complexes. No matter how comprehensive, how "far afield" the sphere of exploration may be, what it is brought to bear upon determines whether the exploration is analytical. Since every complex which is a complex for judgment is *ipso facto* discriminated, the analytical process further discriminates the traits of the complex as an integrity, and inevitably elaborates these traits by approaching them from different angles.

The integrity of a complex is what distinguishes that complex from others in the midst of its relation to them. Analysis is one way of pursuing the definitional process methodically. The given complex, like all others, is an order of subaltern complexes and is subaltern in another order. It may be the kind of complex that is significantly said to have parts, or to be part of another. And we are able now to see more precisely why this whole–part aspect of it is of no essential pertinence to analysis. For its integrity may be progressively judged through exploring the whole of which it is a part as well as through exploring its parts. If, for instance, the complex we are analyzing is student apathy, we explore its integrity not merely by tracing the feelings which are part of it, but by studying the social climate, the institutions, the community of which the condition is itself part. Either of these, whether part or whole, is a constituent, a constituting trait. Where our exploratory concern, then, is with the complex *as* an integrity, it is with the complex as constituted, and is an analytical process. Where, on the other hand, the same complex is judged as contributing to or bearing upon (i.e., as constituting) another, our concern may be not only with its relevance to the integrity of another, but with another which is more extensive or inclusive than it. The latter emphasis, which is actually a special one within the non-analytical emphasis, would (in the classical framework that we are re-defining) be called "synthetic." We can replace this notoriously confusing term by the term "co-ordinative," which not only allows us to suggest query that treats a given complex instrumentally and non-analytically rather than intrinsically, but also allows us to suggest query that treats it as instrumental in a particular direction, namely, to the merging or building of complexes (orders). In the co-ordinative function of query, then, as differentiated from the analytical, we are concerned not with a given complex as constituted, but with that complex as prospectively relevant to (as constituting) a different, and perhaps more inclusive, complex and order. A philosophic generalization, for example, is co-ordinative in so far as it finds diverse complexes to possess a fundamental similarity, or in so far as it explains how ostensibly disparate complexes share location in a given order.

Query (among its many possible sets of alternative paths) may thus dwell (analytically) upon a complex as such, or (co-ordinatively) upon a complex as bearing upon another. The co-ordinative emphasis moves query away from a complex considered as an integrity and toward its ontological environment. Literally, this emphasis *trans*ordinates the complex, considering it as potentially located in another order of prevalence. As we have seen, analysis may entail a search for the ramifications of a complex, for its far-flung relations. But it is analysis in so far as the ramifications are brought to bear upon the given complex as an integrity, in so far as these ramifications serve to define *it* rather than to bring it into the ambit of another.

Poetry embodies both the analytical and the co-ordinative functions of judgment on the exhibitive level. If it does not "make distinctions," it distinguishes traits. But distinguishing traits may consist fully as much in uncovering similarities as in uncovering differences. Every integrity poetically defined is in one respect like every integrity whatever: it has unique traits and traits in common with others. "Thoroughness" is a consideration irrelevant to poetry. For poetry does not explain or classify complexes, or solve problems, or in general accumulate data pertinent to truth-claims and formulae. Repeating a point made earlier: unlike a scientific finding, a poetic finding, whether analytical or co-ordinative, opposes no other findings. Yet there is a poetic counterpart to thoroughness—effective discrimination of many-sidedness. Without this, the role of poetic analysis in poetic query is somehow submerged. We intimated a few pages back that in the arts the analytical process most signicantly takes the form of rotating a complex, delineating it in different perspectives. The integrity of the complex is defined through a plurality of its manifestations. Thus a series of novels by an author concerned recurrently with the same village or culture or level of social life constitutes a type of exhibitive analysis, strategically varying conditions which define a given complex. Repeated portraits of the same person by a single painter, or successive treatments of a traditional theme (e.g., the Crucifixion) by various painters, exemplify essentially the same process of analytical rotation.

Now any perspectival order in which the poet judges the prevalence of a complex perforce exhibits the integrity of that complex. But it does not necessarily exhibit this integrity as a many-sidedness. In other words, poetry always has a minimal analytical aspect in so far as it exposes and defines a constitution of traits, an integrity dealt with as such. But the sense of analytical exploration (for that integrity) is best communicated when there is occasion for the kind of definition that is varied or elaborated to an exceptional degree.

A complex may have a different integrity in each of the interrelated orders where it is located. What emerges from these locations or "roles" is a kind of over-all integrity or contour. The poet may seek to render such a contour in an extended body of work; that is, by rotating the complex in various perspectives. It would seem to be a fair question whether his concern with each ordinal integrity is analytical and his collective concern with the emergent contour co-ordinative, or whether his entire enterprise is a large-scale analysis emphasizing a large-scale integrity. In practice, there is no serious problem of detecting the predominant orientation or of finding both orientations present. But even in an individual poem there is a comparative aspect. More than one perspective is involved: the perspective of the respondent and the perspective of the poem. The poet judges an integrity for a complex which is ordinarily seen as having a different integrity, or which is ordinarily unseen in everyday life. He "distinguishes" traits *both* in the sense of distinguishing a complex *for* those whom he addresses, and in the sense of distinguishing that complex *from* the way it may have been distinguished by them. In this analytical function the poet is not committed to the revelation of inadequacy in other judgments; he is committed solely to the exhibitive definition of a complex considered in its integrity. Once the general principle of analysis is formulated, it is clear that neither in the sciences nor in the arts nor in philosophy must analysis be a "negative" or merely ancillary function.

An analytical function of query is thus congenial to poetry, and even inevitable, as it is in philosophy. Yet the reason we cannot overstate the significance of this truth is that relatively few poems and relatively few works of art in general shape a complex with a sufficiently striking degree of emphasis on the multifariousness of its integrity, or on the plurality and continuity of its integrities. The perspectival rotation in poetry must yield extraordinary manyness in order to be deemed appreciably analytical. This degree of emphasis on the constitution of an integrity can be present in a single poem. The poetic drama is the most frequently encountered setting for the analytical process; its very rationale is to rotate a humanly important complex in diverse postures and situations. Outside the drama, the analytical dimension is found mainly in poems of great length. There are exceptions. For example, Shakespeare's *Venus and Adonis,* only moderately long, is a relentless piece of analytical delineation, one which prompted Coleridge to remark upon its wealth of constituent aspects. The 199 six-line stanzas serve as so many variations on a complex of asymmetrical erotic relatedness and ambiguous feeling.

V

Poetry, as we see, can be defined, with reasonable incompleteness. The definitional process involved is one of circumscribing and enunciating functions. We cannot prove that the unique functions we have attributed to poetry are all there are, or that the functions we have found it to share with other methodic undertakings are all it shares. Poetry may be divine madness, as Plato calls it—inventive deviation from the safely inertial side of human judgment. But it is not alone in this status. In its very uniqueness as a discipline, it is continuous with all the other disciplines that are possessed by query.

NOTES

I

The Apologetic and Eulogistic Tradition

1. William Wordsworth, *Observations Prefixed to the Second Edition of Lyrical Ballads.*
2. Giovanni Boccaccio, *Genealogy of the Gentile Gods*, Bk. xiv, sec. vii, translated by Charles G. Osgood in *Boccaccio on Poetry* (Indianapolis: Bobbs-Merrill, 1956).
3. J. W. Mackail, "The Definition of Poetry" in *Lectures on Poetry* (London: Longmans, Green, 1911).
4. All the Shelley quotations are from *A Defence of Poetry.*
5. S. T. Coleridge, *Biographia Literaria*, Ch. XIV.
6. George Santayana, *Interpretations of Poetry and Religion* (New York: Scribner, 1900), Ch. X.
7. Paul Valéry, "Remarks on Poetry" in *The Art of Poetry*, translated by Denise Folliot (New York: Random House, 1961).
8. William Hazlitt, "On Poetry in General" in *Works*, Vol. V, ed. A. R. Waller and A. Glover.
9. Santayana, *Reason in Art* (New York: Scribner, 1905), Ch. VI. (The next two quotations from Santayana are from the same chapter.)
10. All the quotations from Hegel, in this or any other chapter, are from his posthumous *Aesthetik*, translated by F. P. B. Osmaston as *The Philosophy of Fine Art* (1920), and are to be found between pp. 3 and 59 of Volume IV. They are printed with the permission of the publishers, G. Bell and Sons, Ltd., London.
11. A. C. Bradley, "Poetry for Poetry's Sake" in *Oxford Lectures on Poetry* (London: Macmillan, 1909).

II

Feeling and the "Inner World"

1. J. H. Wheelock, *What Is Poetry?* (New York: Scribner, 1963), Ch. 6.
2. Coleridge, Lectures of 1818, Sec. 1. (See K. Raine, ed. *Samuel Taylor Coleridge*, Baltimore: Penguin Books, 1957.)
3. Santayana, *Interpretations of Poetry and Religion*, Ch. X.
4. Wallace Stevens, # xxvii (part) from "The Man with the Blue Guitar" in *The Collected Poems of Wallace Stevens*. Copyright 1935 by Alfred A. Knopf, Inc., and reprinted with the publisher's permission.
5. W. B. Yeats, "Running to Paradise" in *Responsibilities* (Churchtown, Dumdrum: The Cuala Press, 1914).
6. Yeats, *The Resurrection* (from the last eight lines) in *The Collected Plays of W. B. Yeats*. Copyright 1934 by Macmillan and Co. London. Quoted by permission of The Macmillan Co., New York, and by permission of M. B. Yeats and the Macmillan Companies of London and Canada.
7. Quotations from Mill are from the two essays "What Is Poetry?" and "The Two Kinds of Poetry," mostly the former. See either *Mill's Essays on Literature and Society*, ed. J. B. Schneewind, (New York: Collier, 1965) or *John Stuart Mill: Literary Essays*, ed. E. Alexander (Indianapolis: Bobbs-Merrill, 1967).
8. A poem by Onakatomi Yoshinobu (*c.* 900), translated by Arthur Waley in *Japanese Poetry: The Uta* (London, 1919). Quoted by permission of the publisher, Lund Humphries Publishers, Ltd., and Alison Waley.
9. John Keats, Sonnet "Why Did I Laugh Tonight?"
10. Keats, "Ode to Psyche," V.
11. Keats, "Ode to a Nightingale," V.
12. All quotations from Eastman are from "What Poetry Is" in *Enjoyment of Poetry* (New York: Scribner, 1939).
13. F. A. Pottle, *The Idiom of Poetry* (Bloomington: Indiana University Press, 1963), Ch. IV.
14. Lascelles Abercrombie, "Diction and Experience" in *Theory of Poetry* (New York: Harcourt, Brace, 1926).
15. A. N. Whitehead, *Science and the Modern World* (New York: Macmillan, 1925), Ch. V.
16. Whitehead, *Adventures of Ideas* (New York: Macmillan, 1933), Ch. XI.

17. Whitehead, *Process and Reality* (New York: Macmillan, 1929), Pt. II, Ch. VIII.
18. Keats, "Ode to a Nightingale," VII.
19. Arthur Rimbaud, Letter to Paul Demeny. (See O. Bernard, ed. *Rimbaud*, Baltimore: Penguin Books, 1962.)

III

The Idea of Concreteness

1. Philip Wheelwright, *The Burning Fountain* (Bloomington: Indiana University Press, 1968), 2nd ed., pp. 35, 34, 60.
2. Samuel Alexander, *Beauty and Other Forms of Value* (London: Macmillan, 1933), Ch. VI.
3. T. S. Eliot. From "The Dry Salvages" in *Four Quartets*. Copyright, 1943, by T. S. Eliot, copyright, 1971, by Esme Valerie Eliot. Reprinted by permission of Harcourt Brace Jovanovich, Inc., Reprinted also from *Collected Poems 1909–1962* by permission of Faber and Faber, Ltd., London.
4. Santayana, *Reason in Art*, Ch. VI.
5. Lucretius, *De Rerum Natura*, II, 217–24. Verse translation by William E. Leonard published as the book *Of the Nature of Things* by Lucretius. Everyman's Library edition, 1950. Published by E. P. Dutton & Co., Inc., and used with their permission, as well as the permission of the British publishers, J. M. Dent and Sons, Ltd. The original Latin:

> corpora cum deorsum rectum per inane feruntur
> ponderibus propriis, incerto tempore ferme
> incertisque locis spatio depellere paulum,
> tantum quod momen mutatum dicere possis.
> quod nisi declinare solerent, omnia deorsum,   .
> imbris uti guttae, caderent per inane profundum,
> nec foret offensus natus nec plaga creata
> principiis. ita nihil umquam Natura creasset.

6. Method, as here understood, is not to be equated with the mechanical application of rules, or with the routine employment of standardized procedures; these are at best limited aspects of methodic activity. See my *The Concept of Method*.
7. Santayana, *Reason in Art*, Ch. VI.

8. Whitehead, *Modes of Thought* (New York: Macmillan, 1938), Lect. VII.
9. Osmaston translation, p. 59 (see Note 10 to Chapter I).
10. Shakespeare, Sonnet 33.
11. Shakespeare, *3 King Henry VI*, II, v, 1–13.
12. Shakespeare, *The Phoenix and Turtle*, Stanzas 1, 3, 4, 6–12.
13. Aristotle, *Poetics* 1462 b, *Metaphysics* 1016 b. Aristotle's reason for regarding the circle as most truly one is that it is "whole and complete"—introducing worse problems and further begging the question.

IV

On Various Contrasts of Poetry and Prose

1. Eliot, Introduction to Valéry's *The Art of Poetry*.
2. Valéry, "Remarks on Poetry" in *The Art of Poetry*.
3. J. W. Mackail, "The Definition of Poetry" in *Lectures on Poetry*.
4. Coleridge, *Biographia Literaria*, Ch. XIV.
5. Coleridge, Lectures and Notes of 1818, Sec. 1.
6. See Note 10 to Chapter I.
7. John Dewey, *Art as Experience* (New York: Minton, Balch, 1934), Ch. X.
8. W. M. Urban, *Language and Reality* (London: Allen and Unwin, 1939), Ch. X.

V

Poetic Judgment and Poetic Query

1. Robert Browning, *The Ring and the Book*, XII.
2. Browning, *The Inn Album*, IV.
3. An Egyptian poem of the 12th Dynasty. The translation is in *The Beginnings of Civilization* by Sir Leonard Woolley, which is Volume One, Part II of *The History of Mankind* (Part I is by Jacquetta Hawkes). Copyright 1963 by UNESCO. Reprinted by permission of Harper & Row, Publishers, Inc., and by permission of George Allen & Unwin, Ltd., London.
4. Arthur Symons, Introduction to Everyman's Library edition of *Biographia Literaria* (London: J. M. Dent and Sons, 1906, 1949).
5. P. B. Shelley, Letter to Maria Gisborne, lines 202–208.
6. Whitehead, *Science and the Modern World*, Ch. V.

7. Might it not be said that Greek tragic poetry, for example, seeks "resolutions"; that the resolutions express themselves in the cathartic process? There may indeed be resolutions of some kind in all tragic poetry. But it is not poetic *wonder* that is resolved or mitigated. On the contrary, after the resolution the poetic wonder is intensified. The tragedy resolves the perplexity, the relational obscurity, of a human situation. The wonder is achieved by the poetic judgment of what thus *prevails* (see Chapter VI). Catharsis, in the last analysis, is a species of clarification. Through exhibitive clarification, the tragic poet generates wonder anew.

8. John Donne, "The Good-morrow," lines 15–18.

9. J.-P. Sartre, *What Is Literature?* translated by Bernard Frechtman (New York: Harper & Row, 1965), Ch. I.

10. Alexander Pope, *Essay on Man,* Epistle III.

11. Pope, *Moral Essays,* Epistle III.

12. William Blake, "Mock on, Mock on, Voltaire, Rousseau."

VI

Ontological Parity and the Sense of Prevalence

1. See P. O. Kristeller, "The Modern System of the Arts," in his *Renaissance Thought II* (New York: Harper & Row, 1965).

2. Eliot, "The Music of Poetry," in *On Poetry and Poets* (New York: Noonday Press, 1961).

3. W. H. Auden, *The Dyer's Hand* (New York: Random House, n.d.), Pt. II.

4. A desert mirage, we say, appears to be a body of water but really is not. But we can also say that a given diagram appears to represent a mirage but really does not. And we can say, of a body of water, that it appears to be a spring but really is not.

5. Thus "a sense of" as here used can apply both to what has traditionally and vaguely been called sense-perception ("a sense of redness", "a sense of color") and to sensing of the less familiar kind ("a sense of what you are saying", "a sense of ontological parity"). See above, Chapter II, Section iv.

6. It is not metaphysically accurate to say that any natural complex merely as such and under any conditions—in all respects—prevails. It prevails in so far as its integrity does exclude traits which would modify that integrity. To the extent that the complex *admits* or *allows* such traits, it cannot be said to prevail: to this

extent and in this respect, it is not a prevalence but an *alescence*. Prevalence and alescence are the exhaustive natural dimensions. See my *Metaphysics of Natural Complexes*.

7. A poem by Saigyō Hōshi (1118–1190), translated by Arthur Waley in *Japanese Poetry: The Uta* (London, 1919). Quoted by permission of the publisher, Lund Humphries Publishers, Ltd., and Alison Waley.

8. William Carlos Williams, "The Lion" in his *Collected Later Poems*. Copyright 1949 by William Carlos Williams. Reprinted by permission of New Directions Publishing Corporation.

9. Nicanor Parra, "Young Poets" ("Jovenes") translated by Miller Williams in Parra's *Poems and Antipoems*. Copyright 1967 by Nicanor Parra. Reprinted by permission of New Directions Publishing Corporation.

The original Spanish:

> Escriban lo que quieran.
> En el estilo que les parezca mejor.
> Ha pasado demasiada sangre bajo los puentes
> Para seguir creyendo
> Que sólo se puede seguir un camino.
>
> En poesía se permite todo.
>
> A condición expresa
>   por cierto
> De superar la página en blanco.

10. Marianne Moore, "The Fish" (six of the eight stanzas) in her *Collected Poems*. Copyright 1935 by Marianne Moore. Reprinted by permission of the Macmillan Company, New York. Reprinted also from *The Complete Poems* by permission of Faber and Faber, Ltd., London.

11. Auden, *The Dyer's Hand*, Pt. II.

12. Ezra Pound, "The Garden" in his *Personae*. Copyright 1926 by Ezra Pound. Reprinted by permission of New Directions Publishing Corporation. Reprinted also from *Collected Shorter Poems* by permission of Faber and Faber, Ltd., London.

13. Psalm 137.

14. Henry King, "The Double Rock."

15. Charles Baudelaire, "A Carrion" ("Une Charogne"), Stanzas 1, 2, 5, 10–12. Translated by Allen Tate. Reprinted from Tate's *The Swimmers and Other Selected Poems*, copyright 1970, by permis-

sion of The Swallow Press, Chicago. (The translation, apparently composed in the '20s, appears in Mark Van Doren's *Anthology of World Poetry*, 1928, and in *The Swimmers* contains a few verbal changes.)

The original French:

> Rappelez-vous l'objet que nous vimes, mon âme,
> Ce beau matin d'été si doux:
> Au détour d'un sentier une charogne infâme
> Sur un lit semé de cailloux,
>
> Les jambes en l'air, comme une femme lubrique
> Brûlante et suant les poisons,
> Ouvrait d'une façon nonchalante et cynique
> Son ventre plein d'exhalaisons.
>
> . . .
>
> Les mouches bourdonnaient sur ce ventre putride,
> D'où sortaient de noirs bataillons
> De larves, qui coulaient comme un épais liquide
> Le long de ces vivants haillons.
>
> . . .
>
> —Et pourtant vous serez semblable à cette ordure,
> A cette horrible infection,
> Étoile de mes yeux, soleil de ma nature,
> Vous, mon ange et ma passion!
>
> Oui! telle vous serez, ô la reine des grâces,
> Après les dernier sacrements,
> Quand vous irez, sous l'herbe et les floraisons grasse
> Moisir parmi les ossements.
>
> Alors, ô ma beauté! dites à la vermine
> Qui vous mangera de baisers,
> Que j'ai gardé la forme et l'essence divine
> De mes amours décomposés!

VII

Knowledge, Actuality, and Analysis in Poetry

1. Eliot, Introduction to Marianne Moore's *Selected Poems* (New York: Macmillan, 1935).
2. Susanne K. Langer, *Feeling and Form* (New York: Scribner, 1953), pp. 217, 257, 258, 217, 211, 212, 214.

INDEX

Abercrombie, L., 43
Abstraction, 63 ff., 71
Active judgment, 97 ff., 148
Actuality, 16, 51, 53, 60 ff., 153–9
Alexander, E., 175
Alexander, S., 51, 57 ff.
Alliteration, 117, 129
Analysis, 51, 59, 159–73
Ancient Mariner, The, 107
Aquinas, Thomas, 78
Aristotle, 13, 17, 55 f., 71, 73, 79, 165
Art, 15 ff., 101, 108
Articulation, 102, 107–16, 127, 137
Assent, 127
Assertive judgment, 97 ff.
Assonance, 117
Auden, W. H., 122, 138
Augustine, St., 145

Baudelaire, Charles, 179
Belief, 29, 36, 107
Bergson, Henri, 163
Bernard, O., 176
Bible, 73, 82
Biographia Literaria, 82
Blake, William, 178
Boccaccio, Giovanni, 8
Botticelli, Sandro, 34
Bradley, A. C., 19

Brothers Karamazov, The, 130
Browning, Robert, 177

Catharsis, 178
Cézanne, Paul, 34
Coleridge, S. T., 10 ff., 24, 73, 80 ff., 107 f., 118, 173
Communication, 19, 141
Concreteness, Ch. III, 71
Consciousness, 82 ff., 89 ff.
Criticism, 101

Definition, 69, 106
Description, 105 f.
Dewey, John, 48, 85
Donne, John, 178
Drama, 30, 51, 173

Eastman, Max, 40–44, 76
Eliot, T. S., 73, 119, 152
Eloquence, 30, 142, 145
Empedocles, 73
Essay on Man, 47
Ethics (Spinoza), 78
Eulogism, Ch. I
Euripides, 156
Exhibitive judgment, 97–116, 123
Existence, 52, 55
Experience, 4, Ch. II *passim,* 63, 89 f., 155
Explicitness, 18, 20

Expression, 17 ff., 95

Faerie Queene, The, 134
Fancy, 25 f., 109
Feeling, Ch. II, 99 f.
Fictions, 7, 125, 157
Fielding, Henry, 144
Folliot, D., 174
Frechtman, B., 178
Frege, Gottlob, 168

Glover, A., 174
Goethe, J. W. von, 157 f.

Hazlitt, William, 13
Hegel, G. W. F., 13–20, 65–72,
    82–4
Homer, 73, 82
Hooker, Richard, 48
Hume, David, 165

Iliad, 134
Image, 47 f., 68 f.
Imagination, 4, 9 ff., 17, 65, 83,
    154 f.
Immediacy, 42, 61, 64 f.
In Memoriam, 109
Individual, 55, 64 f., 91 f.
Integrity, 91 f., 169 ff.
Interrogative temper, 110 ff.

James, William, 55
Joyce, James, 144
Judgment, 3, 92–102

Kant, Immanuel, 11
Keats, John, 38
King, Henry, 179
Knowledge, 14, 16, 148–52
Kristeller, P. O., 178

Langer, S. K., 154
Language, 9, 16 ff., 63, 74 ff.,
    99, 122 f.
Leonard, W. E., 176
Locke, John, 40, 48, 165
Lucretius, 176

Mackail, J. W., 8
MacLeish, Archibald, 111
Mantegna, Andrea, 34
Marlowe, Christopher, 157
Meaning, 75 ff., 97, 102, 111 ff.
Metaphor, 9, 129
Metonymy, 129
Mill, J. S., 29–38, 44, 142, 167
Milton, John, 47, 108
Moore, G. E., 161
Moore, Marianne, 179
Music, 17, 20, 34, 74, 117 ff.

Natural complex, 103 f.
Nature, 104
Novelist, 29 f., 41, 59, 123, 143 ff.

On Liberty, 167
Onakatomi Yoshinobu, 175
Ontological parity and priority,
    56, 103, Ch. VI
Order, 9, 88 ff., 157
Organic, 13, 51, 59 f., 64 ff.
Osgood, C. G., 174
Osmaston, F. P. B., 174

Painting, 17, 20, 31 ff., 117
Paradise Lost, 47
Parra, Nicanor, 179
Particular, 50, 61 f., 64
Paul, St., 145
Peirce, C. S., 168
Perspective, 89, 171 f.

Philosophy, 16, 41, 43, 62 f., 79, 159
Plato, 145 ff., 167, 173
Pleasure, 9, 80
Poe, E. A., 74, 119
Pope, Alexander, 47, 108, 114
Possibility, 26, 53, 62, 156
Pottle, F. A., 41
Pound, Ezra, 152, 179
Prevalence, 129–45, 178 f.
Prose, 14, 41, 51, 62 f., Ch. IV
Proust, Marcel, 144

Quality, 40 ff.
Query, 108–16, 153, 155, 170

Racine, J. B., 156
Raine, K., 175
Reality, 4, 123 ff.
Reason, 9
Relevance, 91
Religion, 16, 43, 144 f.
Rhyme, 117, 129
Rimbaud, Arthur, 48, 113 f.
Russell, Bertrand, 164

Saigyō Hōshi, 179
Santayana, George, 13 ff., 27 ff., 58, 63, 120
Sartre, J.-P., 113 ff.
Schneewind, J. B., 175
Science, 10, 29, 35 f., 73, 79 f., 83 ff., 96 f., 109 ff., 155
Sense, 17, 45 ff.
Shakespeare, William, 68, 173
Shelley, P. B., 8, 9, 17, 73, 86, 108
Sidney, Philip, 86, 104
Simmel, Georg, 48
Simples, 104
Sitwell, Edith, 41

Speech, 16 f., 117, 120 ff., 125
Spinoza, Baruch, 78
Stevens, Wallace, 175
Symons, Arthur, 108
Symposium, 167

Tate, Allen, 179
Tennyson, Alfred, 108 f.
Tom Jones, 144
Translation, 79 f., 101
Tropes, 129
Truth, 14, 16, 31 ff., 86

Ulysses, 144
Unity, 11, 13, 66, 71 f.
Urban, W. M., 86
Utterance, 3, 92–6

Valéry, Paul, 13, 75–81
Van Doren, Mark, 180
Venus and Adonis, 173
Verse, 73

Waley, Arthur, 175, 179
Waller, A. R., 174
What Is Literature?, 113
Wheelock, J. H., 175
Wheelwright, Philip, 50, 58 ff.
Whitehead, A. N., 44–8, 51, 56, 63, 108 f.
Whole man, 12 ff.
Williams, M., 179
Williams, W. C., 179
Wittgenstein, Ludwig, 161, 164
Wonder, 11 ff., 141, 178
Woolley, L., 177
Wordsworth, William, 8, 29, 73, 108

Yeats, W. B., 175

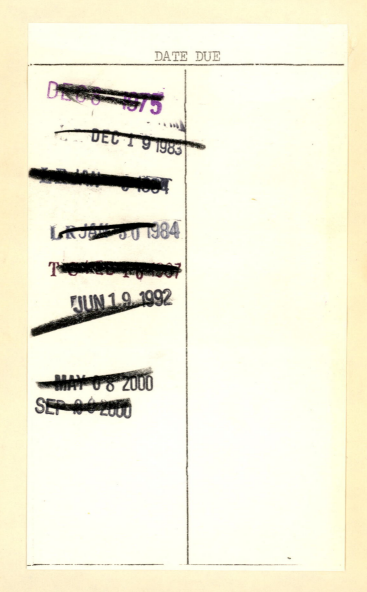